Prayers *to an* Evolutionary God

Prayers *to an* Evolutionary

God

William Cleary

Afterword by Diarmuid O'Murchu

Walking Together, Finding the Way
SKYLIGHT PATHS® Publishing
Nashville, Tennessee

Prayers to an Evolutionary God
© 2004 by William Cleary
Afterword © 2004 by Diarmuid O'Murchu

Requests to the Publisher for permission should be addressed to Turner Publishing Company, 4507 Charlotte Avenue, Suite 100, Nashville, Tennessee, (615) 255-2665, fax (615) 255-5081, E-mail: submissions@turnerpublishing.com.

Grateful acknowledgment is given for permission to use "Remembering Loveliness" by Mary Goergen, OSF, used by permission.

Library of Congress Cataloging-in-Publication Data
Cleary, William.
Prayers to an evolutionary God / William Cleary, afterword by Diarmuid O'Murchu.
p. cm.
Includes bibliographical references and index.
ISBN 1-59473-006-7 (hardcover)
ISBN 978-1-68336-551-8 (paperback)
1. Prayers. 2. Process theology. I. Title.
BL560.C54 2004
204'.33—dc22

2004001518

SkyLight Paths Publishing is creating a place where people of different spiritual traditions come together for challenge and inspiration, a place where we can help each other understand the mystery that lies at the heart of our existence.

SkyLight Paths sees both believers and seekers as a community that increasingly transcends traditional boundaries of religion and denomination—people wanting to learn from each other, *walking together, finding the way.*

10   9   8   7   6   5   4   3   2

Manufactured in the United States of America

SkyLight Paths, "Walking Together, Finding the Way" and colophon are trademarks of LongHill Partners, Inc., registered in the U.S. Patent and Trademark Office.

Walking Together, Finding the Way
Published by SkyLight Paths Publishing
An Imprint of Turner Publishing Company
4507 Charlotte Avenue, Suite 100
Nashville, TN 37209
Tel: (615) 255-2665
www.skylightpaths.com

To two beloved friends

and friends of the Earth:

prophetic Jane Blewett,

seer in the dark,

and ingenious genius

Lou Niznik,

who has always worked

as fast and as hard

as he could.

Contents

> The evolutionary story requires that we listen attentively
> to the evolving process transpiring over billions of years.
> Our failure to attend to this expansive vision may well
> be the major cause of the alienation and estrangement
> that we often experience in our daily lives.
>
> —Diarmuid O'Murchu

> My religion consists of a humble admiration of the
> illimitable superior spirit.
>
> —Albert Einstein

> I have grave doubts that the story of evolution can be
> reduced to one cycle, commencing about twelve billion
> years ago and culminating some five to ten billion years
> from now. It's all too neat for the creativity of divine
> becoming.
>
> —Diarmuid O'Murchu

> The important thing is not to stop questioning.
> Curiosity has its own reason for existing.
>
> —Albert Einstein

III. Prayers of Ambiguity   85

> Darkness...often characterizes the spiritual journey.
> —Diarmuid O'Murchu

> The most beautiful experience we can have is the mysterious.
> —Albert Einstein

IV. Prayers of Intimacy   127

> Spirit-power is the ultimate force field that generates and maintains the creativity of the cosmos.
> —Diarmuid O'Murchu

> I belong to the ranks of devoutly religious men.
> —Albert Einstein

Introduction
Close Encounters with Teilhard de Chardin

In the fall of 1961 when I rang the doorbell at the Jesuit house on West 108th Street in New York, the home of *America* magazine, I was welcomed in by the gray-haired superior himself. My newly minted Roman collar certified me for entrance. The nonstop flight from Kansas was my first as a priest.

The superior took my bag, then led me past brightly lit editorial offices to an ancient elevator, and we ascended to the fifth floor. On our way to a front room where I was to live, we passed the classic Halsman photograph of Teilhard de Chardin mounted on the hallway wall. "Teilhard lived in this room," said the priest, setting my bag down, "till he died six years ago."

My jaw dropped: I had just read the great paleontologist's most beloved book, *The Divine Milieu,* twice in one day. No author on earth could have been more in the forefront of my consciousness. I was suddenly to live where he had lived—and died. It was spooky.

The brokenhearted, unpublished genius Teilhard de Chardin—the "most significant theologian since St. Paul," according to geologian Thomas Berry—was to haunt me the rest of my life. Why? Not just for his scientific achievement, prophetic poetry, and posthumous fame (he made the cover of *Time*), but for modeling nonconformity and personal freedom. At a time when it was theologically suicidal, especially for Jesuit priests, his God was unapologetically an evolutionary God.

What kind of God is that? You will, I hope, find that out— if you do not already know—in this book. An evolutionary God is the one whose fingerprints and embraces and music we find in the evolutionary patterns in the unfinished world around us, the elusive mother and inventor of this ever-changing milieu. It is a God who pretends—for some purpose we do not comprehend—not even to exist, but whom we can reach out for and give thanks to, if we wish—as most of our race has done throughout its history.

The purpose of this creation—if we harmonize with the ideas of Teilhard de Chardin and of process theologians since his time—is beauty, adventure, the challenge of soul-building, of connectedness discovered and created. Teilhard made it all wildly exciting for religious people by suggesting that it is religion that completes—not competes with—evolution. Our evolutionary God is above all a God of desire and love, of every kind of love we know and of loves we cannot know, a God of colossal wisdom, inventiveness, and risk; a God utterly beyond us, within us, and ahead of us.

Deep Water

I feel I am swimming in very deep water here. I had the same feeling once as I floated out on the surface of a lake they told me was "a mile deep," in a rain-filled volcano in Nicaragua—that experience gave me a similar sense of dread and inadequacy. I have not read all the works of Teilhard de Chardin. Nor have I any personal expertise in the field of evolution. I rely mostly on one book, a brilliant synthesis of science and spirit written by the Irish priest-psychologist Diarmuid O'Murchu, titled *Evolutionary Faith*, and I cite him on almost every page.

My own specialty is turning thoughts—in this case largely O'Murchu's—into prayers, inventing words for "speaking into the silence," in Karl Rahner's expression. That's what *prayer* is, in my usage: a substantial thought turned into "something to do." Religious people, I have found, thrive on things to do rather than theological ideas: they want to visit a shrine, or light a candle, or sing a hymn, or spin a prayer wheel. This book gives them something to do about the astonishing revelations of mystery found in evolutionary physics: say a prayer.

The part titles Prayers of Listening, of Questioning, of Ambiguity, and, finally, of Intimacy roughly correspond to an idealized spiritual lifetime. Infancy is a time of listening and imitation, childhood an endless explosion of importunate questions. Spiritual adulthood may then go through adolescent uncertainty en route not to certitude but to an adult surrender to ambiguity that is tolerant and open. Finally, like facing real death, our spiritual life may arrive at the ripe intimacy of an indefinable "I–Thou" hopefulness. Of course, moods may switch us back and forth between these spiritual styles all through life.

Verbal prayers make sense, I think, if you know in advance that talking to God is like talking to your dog. You say human words to your dog, but he pretty much ignores that in favor of how you smell. Similarly, whatever divinity there is hears your words of prayer but very likely ignores all you say in favor of the aroma of your heart: your kindness, your compassion—for both your own poor soul and for your have-not brothers and sisters in the world. But the words of your prayer do matter to you: they give shape to your thoughts; they warm and give color to your soul and spur you to a focused listening.

Ideas about Prayer

Old-fashioned ideas about prayer can be misleading but they are seldom harmful—unless we begin to blame ourselves for not influencing God more. "Pray hard," people say, forgetting that God is already all-compassionate, and that no amount of petitioning can bring about change. People make nine days of devotions, say the rosary over and over, make pilgrimages, visit shrines and saintly people—but you can't pinch God. Goodness and generosity flow from the Evolutionary Mystery constantly, and the most appropriate prayers are words and gestures of surrender, praise, gratitude, and awe.

We may choose to remember God at meals and give thanks. Perhaps we say a prayer as we drift off into sleep. In crisis we might find ourselves praying: "God help me!" All these are natural moments for prayer and perfectly innocent. But within the narrative of evolution, says O'Murchu, "we find ourselves appropriating quite a different understanding of what God and the divine life-force are all about." He implies the need for a whole new evolutionary spirituality.

Why cultivate an evolutionary perspective? We may think of it as something like the pleasure of living in the mountains. Living in mountainous country is fun partly because you can always see where you are. "Fourteen miles from Mount Helena" is a location for yourself you wouldn't know of if Helena were flat instead of up there looking down on you like a white-topped elder. Discovering yourself in a larger and unfamiliar perspective is enlightening too and helps you define your name in a sense: know who you are—because where you are often tells you who you are. We name ourselves Americans partly because of where we are. Similarly, seeing earth from outer space redefines our global self-identity forever.

Star Dust, Star Children

And so—in the Universe Story—knowing ourselves as children and grandchildren of the Big Bang gives us illuminating and thrilling self-knowledge and perspective, a little like living in the mountains. It's intriguing to know yourself encircled by the mountainous events of evolution and to be a child of light, alive like other living things. Why alive? Because there are stars (we learn in O'Murchu), and one of them, the sun, has warmed you and your kind into existence as an alive and conscious earthen person. Where there's light, there's life, he reports. We are, in this perspective, the children of a star, of the sun.

If you are inclined to pray at all (you need not), these prayers place you within the mind-blowing narrative of evolution rather than simply in a cloud of bewilderment or, worse, within the male-dominant story of the Garden of Eden, a place increasingly inhospitable to modern spirituality. Prayer in this book is considered as a kind of luxury, an enrichment of a contemplative life, a privilege—never a request for something from God, or an attempt to affect reality in some way: stop a war, heal a wound, or make it rain.

The Jesuits did not bury Teilhard de Chardin in an unmarked grave, but they did not put his name on it either. I stumbled on the place one icy morning in 1969 in the same spooky way I'd been assigned to his room: on the very anniversary day of his death. I was out early for a troubled walk around the foggy grounds of the Jesuit seminary in Poughkeepsie, New York, thinking with a breaking heart of departing from the Jesuit brotherhood after twenty-two years of membership. My eyes were drawn to the grave because, alone among the hundreds of identical burial sites, flowers—covered now with snow—lay on its grassy bed. Some unknown hand—perhaps during the night—had placed there a dozen long-stemmed irises.

I peered at the gravestone, one of hundreds in that dim seminary churchyard. Engraved there was simply the name "Pierre Teilhard," not his full name. (The affront has since been remedied.) Teilhard had often said whimsically that he wanted to die on an Easter day, and it had come about. By a startling coincidence, the day I found his grave was another Easter.

Easter is, of course, not a Christian invention. In fact, there is a danger that a theological celebration could alienate us from the real miracles of springtime that the Evolutionary God amazes us with year after year. In fact, there is no more apt paradigm for the continuous eastering we call evolution than a springtime of ever-new wonders. May it ever be so.

1
Prayers of Listening

The evolutionary story requires that we listen attentively to the evolving process transpiring over billions of years. Our failure to attend to this expansive vision may well be the major cause of the alienation and estrangement that we often experience in our daily lives.

—Diarmuid O'Murchu

My religion consists of a humble admiration of the illimitable superior spirit.

—Albert Einstein

How do you expect to keep your powers of hearing when you never want to listen? That God shall have time for you you seem to take as much for granted as that you cannot have time for God.

—Dag Hammarskjöld

Sometimes we find the numinous, the sacred, at the center of nature or the life force, or at the heart of a vivid human experience. That may be as close to "God" as we may ever come. For science buffs, nothing is more awesome than the mysteries—the constants, the forces, the elegance—of physical reality.

Question: Dare we—like monks praying to the Eucharistic bread in another era—*speak* to that sacred center? Is it personal enough to hear us, or to even possibly rejoice that we have found it, and found it awesome?

It seems a worthwhile risk, and we take it constantly here. Nothing is lost if we are wrong and the sacred turns out to be simply impersonal at last—but of course we shall never know. In the meantime it makes for an interesting faith experiment or spiritual "ropes test." We give it trust—hoping a new burst of interior confidence may be the result.

Also in this way we fall in with the choice of most of the human race throughout its history. They addressed prayers to the sacred. Foolish, self-deluding choice, some may say, but more than likely, say the majority, a wise experiment. Spiritual guides for the most part would say, "If it helps, do it, try it."

The eighty prayers in this book are built on the brilliant scientific and theological synthesis titled *Evolutionary Faith* by Diarmuid O'Murchu, who also wrote the Afterword. His understanding of evolution is Darwinian, as hugely expanded by the so-called process theology of Alfred North Whitehead and Teilhard de Chardin. If it helps, try it.

1   Toward the Future
—In Hopeful Times

The future is full of promise, Holy Mystery,
if only because we discern your forces of evolution
at work everywhere.
Every opening daffodil, every growing child,
every glimmer of human enlightenment,
every bodily process of healing
tells us the future is not fearsome but is full of potential.
Your face is hidden, your name unknown;
still we turn to you in faith and confidence.
Creating Evolutionary Spirit,
we hear your comforting voice
in the steady music of the unfolding creation,
in harmonies and dissonances of the world around us
into which we pour our humble efforts.
We give thanks to exist,
and to be in some way the joy of your heart.
Amen.

The Episcopal bishop John Shelby Spong explains that for him prayer is "sitting self-consciously in the presence of God until that presence is part of who you are." He wrote this line among others that summed up his views on prayer for an Internet chat room. His other remarks are equally arresting. "Prayer is facing who you are with nonillusory honesty." "Prayer is filling the world and especially those you love with the power of your own positive energy, your life force—which may well be part of who or what God is."

When we put Spong's profound wisdom into the narrative of evolution, we see instantly how important prayer may be, how, through a personal spiritual practice, we can become involved in the evolutionary process as it affects the world around us. Our personal prayer life brings the divine presence into our consciousness, and we carry that presence forward wherever we go.

According to the O'Murchu synthesis, in prehistoric times it may have been in "dancing, chanting, and drumming that we spent most of our time in dialogue with our creative Gods." We enjoy the music that reflects in our judgment "the sound of the world." Gregorian chant is beloved by monks because it is orderly, predictable, and reverent, just like their world. In contrast, in many ways modern jazz reflects a world concept full of improvisation and purposeful dissonance: an evolutionary world.

2   *Enlivening Spirit*
—When Longing to Pray

We turn to you, Enlivening Spirit; we listen to you
because we find it natural and congenial to do so,
even though we are aware
that you must understand us perfectly without our words.
You know us so well
because you create us every moment,
every part of our bodies and minds,
our imaginations and our life,
our whole evolving being, promise and future.
But the urge to be at prayer,
to make your presence and voice
the object of our thoughts:
this is your creation too.
To pray to you is simply to be ourselves
conscious of your reality,
which escapes us when we attend to other things.
But alert to our center, "centered,"
we find your holy presence like a fire
in the middle of a human circle,
like the energies at the center of every atom
or the meaning at the center of life.
That fire is You, calling us into existence, into evolution,
and into faith.
Our prayers, halting and awkward as they are,
are our occasional response,
utterly innate, natural, and as unheroic as breathing
or heartbeat:
simply our full self, aware and in awe,
often wordless.
Hear our prayer.
Amen.

Evolutionary faith works in different ways for different people. It will gradually have its effect, according to O'Murchu, on the way religious services are conducted. Over time, religious leaders will learn to speak from within a larger world, and will often bring natural events—the movement of the stars, the changing of the seasons, the threats to the environment—into their spiritual perspective. Individuals may find themselves deeply in tune with the natural rather than with the supernatural.

However, the need for spirituality and prayer remains ambiguous and a matter of choice. We will never cease to find ourselves deep in the sea of the unknown, not really knowing if speaking human words into the great mystery makes sense or not. Spirituality can be helped by metaphor here, moving from the known to the unknown.

We may have had a good experience of a human mother. We then think of the earth as "mother" or even the Holy Mysterious itself as "Mother" or divine womb. Our God may seem personal or impersonal or extrapersonal. What matters is that we take the broadest possible perspective, and find enlightenment in our meditations. Teilhard de Chardin said: "You are not a human being in search of a spiritual experience. You are a spiritual being immersed in a human experience." It's a perspective worth considering.

3

Boundless Sea
—Looking Ahead

Boundless Sea of Love and Energy,
our future and our God,
may all your dreams for us come true:
your steady motherlike imaginings,
and your fatherly hopes,
your creative purposes evident everywhere in the world.
Guide us to our truest selves,
co-creators with you of this environment.
Persuade us to be worthy inheritors
of the astonishing evolving reality in which we live:
appreciators of the daytime in all its colors and aromas,
admirers of the heavens at night,
reverent caretakers of our generous green earth,
respectful of everything alive—
especially of our fellow humans
in all their bewildering diversity.
May it be so.

The womb can be a helpful paradigm for finding meaning in life. This uniquely feminine organ, in which human life is begun, should mark women for unique reverence. Catholic priest and self-identified "geologian" Thomas Berry says that in terms of saving the planet "the return of the feminine" is the most important movement of our time. He calls it a return because he assumes—as do many other philosophers—that long ago on earth humans believed in a kind of co-natural mutuality of the genders. That feminine return—to essential equality and reverence, which necessarily requires everywhere the elevation of women's status back to the level of shared leadership and sovereignty—seems to be the only path to survival that the current human race has not tried.

World religious practice can be crucial here because people's experiences of ritual are deep and lasting. If the priest or imam is always male, males will be seen as necessarily superior. If even God is male, all the more deep will be the ritual lesson in the inferiority of the other gender. Domination—of the earth or of each other—is a concept we must learn to live without if we hope to develop the caring virtues necessary for world survival.

A great deal is at stake, and if we find the return of the feminine impossible to bring about, the evolving earth may gradually return to its once lifeless state. This level of failure may seem unthinkable, but it may be all but inevitable unless we listen to the cries of anguish from our poisoned and suffocating earth, and if, in compassionate response, we decide as a human family that has no other habitat, to do something about it.

4   *Womb That Nurtures Us*
—When Re-imaging the Divine

Great Sea of Being in which we live and move,
in reverence we raise our minds to you,
minds that are conscious and memory-rich
with the long history of your undefinable goodness,
your mysterious choice of us individually for human life,
and all the immeasurable blessings
you have heaped upon us,
manufacturing long ago, somewhere among the stars,
the carbon and nitrogen atoms
that make up our very bodies.
You—and the earth—are the universal womb
that nurtures all that is,
the unconditional love we depend on,
our spirit-matrix,
the comforting arms that embrace us always,
the steady hum of your mysterious care.
We give thanks,
inadequate and almost preposterous as that seems.
Amen.

The dark side of life—all the threats to the environment we experience—is not the most crucial in any kind of evolutionary perspective. The brighter side—where new levels of life are invented and survive—combines apparently separate energies together, produces innovations, and endures.

In biological evolution, advances happen at the genetic level as organisms' genes change during reproduction and are passed on to future generations. Sometimes offspring inherit new characteristics that give them survival and reproductive advantages in their particular environment: so the fittest—not the strongest—live on. Cooperation is ultimately more crucial than competition.

In evolution's larger framework—proceeding over millions of years starting from the Big Bang, the trajectory of the unfolding universe is positive as well. In the case of our earth, it has carried us from the chaotic beginnings to life, to locomotion, to consciousness, to elegant diversity, to language and communication and a compassionate earthen communion challenged to become one familylike community.

Traditional religions can be a help. The one God of the Bible suggests instantly this one-human-family concept. The Abrahamic traditions bless us with hundreds of optimistic stories, teachings, and prayers. Once we update its worldview, we may continue to find it helpful and inspiring. The heart of the Bible's message—of an essentially benevolent God—could be a permanent part of our personal theology.

About this process we may be optimistic, living in the hope that the force that has overcome challenges in the past can and will do so again—including the challenge that is global warming and a threatened environment.

The Work of Your Spirit
—In Times of Confidence

Holy God, to really accept the implications of evolution,
to not only surrender to its evidences
but to make it our life's faith,
would mean to name our inclinations
toward change, creativity, and becoming
as the work of your own spirit within us,
guiding our hands.
Our view of the future, then, should become less fearful,
and our attitude toward the earth's well-being
more optimistic.
We hear your mysterious voice in all that is.
We are in good hands.
Be with us, Evolutionary Spirit,
giving us ever-greater desires,
and courage to face an unknown of immense promise.
May it be so.

Evolutionary spirituality thrives on scientific information and takes it to prayer, straight to the great mystery whose presence we may almost feel. Thus a new kind of mysticism in us is born. O'Murchu claims, "a cosmic contemplative lies dormant in us all." Teilhard noted in his journal: "Less and less do I see any difference between research and adoration."

Is there a way to wake up that contemplative, that deeper, dormant you? A daily time for meditation and rumination would seem to be a minimal prerequisite. But basically what we do for prayer can be largely a matter of taste and talent. The human imagination comes in multiple sizes and shapes. Ours may be musical but not spatial—we may quickly hum an original melody for a line of poetry but be unable to sketch a tree. Great actors find it simple to imagine that they are President Lincoln or Queen Elizabeth and easily begin to act as if they were—while others can't begin to do so.

Similarly, there is no required way to pray. We never need to imagine God as a person to whom we may speak words in human language, though many do so. Our lives pray, our choices pray: how we live "speaks to God." Ralph Waldo Emerson wrote to a friend, "What you do speaks so loudly that I cannot hear what you say." The same applies in our contemplative relationship to the Great Mystery. What we do, what we are, prays. When we are in touch with ultimate values, we are the universe at prayer.

6   *Incomprehensible God*
—Searching for God

Holy Sea of Purposeful Energy
in which we live and move and have our being
you really have no divine face that smiles on us,
no hands that distribute blessings or hold us safe,
no physical heart to make you compassionate,
no vibrating tone or language to use for our instruction
or guidance or comforting:
you are total mystery.
We cannot imagine you.
Except that in the material world
which we see and live within,
there are evolving wonders:
astonishing events and cosmic phenomena
and people who, in their awesome beauty and elegance,
take our breath away, leaving us speechless, awed.
These are no doubt your breakthrough points:
there we feel your presence most, your mind everywhere,
your enormous potential and life.
Blessed are we to have found you, incomprehensible God.
Amen.

To say "a story has invented us" is to imagine God not as a person like other persons we know but as a kind of continuous narrative of events: a story, a divinity embedded in and revealed in the Universe Story itself. It blows your mind at first. Perhaps you were comfortable with "God the Father," or even "God the Mystery." Yet, evolutionary thinking invites us beyond, into other metaphorical realms. It convinces us that we know less about God than we may have thought, so new metaphors are needed—musical, aromatic, colorful, pleasuresome—building an image of the divine out of all experiential phenomena.

Spirituality makes other novel demands in our times as well. We also need to strive for a kind of personal transparency where, in some circle of intimacy, we hide nothing, an honesty and a surrender to what is real and true for us, trusting that our companions in the circle will remain faithful to us if only we are honest. This is the way we shall fit ourselves into evolution and its story. That story will then envelop us as we become a self-aware part of it.

O'Murchu puts it this way: "It is not just a matter of reinventing the story; rather, it is about acquiring that openness and transparency whereby we can allow ourselves to be enveloped by the story that has invented us."

7

The Story Invented Us
—For Days of Darkness

Speaking within the darkness of faith,
we bless the Larger Reality that seems to have
invented us.
We long to respond to this miracle, to hear its voice.
May our personal efforts of creativity
contribute to the holy process of unfolding
and bring the future ever closer.
It is a privilege to be alive and have a cosmic task:
to be in fact this moment
the very consciousness and self-consciousness
of the universe.
Blessed is all that exists,
ambiguous in its evolution but full of promise.
Wherever is this reality's center,
we bless it from the periphery,
silent, listening, in awe and gratitude.
So be it.

The stars surround us like a womb, and within that womb we grow toward a maturity we cannot really imagine. After billions of years of nonlife on earth came the almost unthinkable: live beings, entities able to move, feed themselves, digest nourishment, reproduce. Then out of those primitive forms came knowledge, consciousness, caringness, and, finally, altruism and mysticism.

"The womb of stars embraces us," writes author Joy Atkinson. "Remnants of their fiery furnaces pulse through our veins." Certain identifiable elements on this earth, says science, could not have come about on this earth but have to have been formed somewhere else in the cosmos. Ours has been an astonishing journey, a noble, communal pilgrimage in search of the holy. And each of us is a part of it and is now responsible for its continuance and appreciative reception.

8 *Your Supportive Presence*
—In Need of Healing

In every pain and disappointment,
we turn to you, our evolutionary God,
our Higher and Deeper Power, our origin,
remembering your supportive presence
in the lives of those who have walked this path
of exploration before us.
We suspect, as many of them did, that we are a part
of something much larger
than what is apparent to our eyes.
Often we feel that we cannot go forward alone
or even in the companionship of our peers
without the energies that your holy presence gives us.
Be with us then, dear God,
alpha and omega of all that is,
great Everywhere-Spirit in whom we trust.
Amen.

"Evolution is a story that continues to unfold under the mysterious wisdom of our co-creative God," says O'Murchu, "whose strategies always have, and always will, outwit our human and religious desire for neat, predictable outcomes." Some theologians also speak of an ongoing trend toward complexity, "toward more and more intense versions of ordered novelty—that is, toward beauty," in the expression of John Haught. Is all that plausible?

The most successful religions keep it convincingly simple. You feel like a sinner? That's because you are, they say. Perhaps it's not due to something you yourself did wrong but something your ancestors did: "original" sin. You're born with it, defiled by that sin in your mother's womb.

That is a simple explanation. One is tempted to believe it. Alas, some myths wear out their plausibility. The evidence indicates instead that we are born not sinful but totally innocent. And beautiful. Evolutionary forces have produced this symmetry and elegance, and each human child a new beauty, a creative achievement produced by many energies working cooperatively, another awesome and sacred event.

9   *Evolutionary Strategies*
—Feeling Bewildered

Holy Mystery, our relational spirit-creator,
allow us to feel nonplussed
by your evolutionary strategies,
so far beyond our present comprehension.
Our imaginations were shaped by another narrative:
we were taught the myth of divine omnipotence.
But it is not that simple.
You, elusive God,
are not, after all, to blame for every illness
and anomaly on earth,
nor are you alone in charge of the evolution
of its creative potential
or responsible for every outcome.
There is an undeniable randomness at work in creation.
We are ourselves co-creators of life and consciousness,
responsible for part of the co-evolution around us.
But all this is baffling.
Help thou our near disbelief.
Amen.

It is possible to believe in evolution without denying the existence of God. What matters is that we begin our thinking about God not with a book or a lesson from someone, but with the experience we ourselves have of things and events that are awesome—even though they are mysterious and mostly not understood.

"Glory be to God for dappled things," exclaimed the poet Gerard Hopkins. "... For skies of couple-color as a brinded cow,/ for rose-moles all in stipple upon trout that swim...."

The colors on a cow, like the tints in a multicolored sky, seemed unspeakably glorious to Hopkins, as were simple rose-colored markings on swimming trout.

That is where our spiritual beliefs may begin, too, when the poet in us sees something awe-inspiring: the grace of a gray cat, the loving spirit of a three-year-old child. After that, reasoning helps. For instance, we can reason that a Spirit-power driving this glorious evolution is also intelligent and wise and knows creation perfectly, knows us perfectly. To feel "known" and "known perfectly" can then be the beginning of a natural mysticism— where the presence of divinity is felt, and spoken to, or danced to. We may also pray, with Hopkins:

"Glory be to God for dappled [speckled, spotted, freckled, un-predictable, disorderly, random] things." Out of such chance beauty and existential gambling on the part of God evolves the earth's whole future. O'Murchu's book *Evolutionary Faith* states it simply: "Spirit-Power is the driving force of the evolutionary process."

Knowing Us Perfectly
—In Silent Awe

Holy Spirit-Power around us and within us,
knowing us and our past perfectly,
having a dream for us we can't really imagine:
we are in awe of your creation as it lies before our eyes,
a living and elegant world
wherein we each find ourselves conscious and alive,
linked to others of our kind by bonds of love and memory,
in awe of your creative presence and caringness.
What shall we do to respond to this revelation?
Inept seem all our efforts at speech:
so sometimes we are silent.
You are God, the Sea of Being in which we live and move.
Alleluia.
Blessed be your incomprehensible name.
Amen.

Shall we ever harness energy enough to overcome, one by one, the challenges that plague us as a race? Teilhard de Chardin claims what we need is the energy of love: "Someday, after mastering winds, waves, tides and gravity, we shall harness the energy of love; and for the second time in the history of the world, man will have discovered fire."

When the long evolutionary process finally produced consciousness, the possibility of love arose. Consciousness is simply our awareness of ourselves and our ability to think and feel, to reason and discern beauty and truth. That self-awareness is a kind of gateway to many more questions and eventually to wisdom, a massive creative force within the world.

Hope for this outcome is promised in O'Murchu's *Evolutionary Faith.* "If Spirit-Power is the ultimate force field that generates and maintains the creativity of the cosmos, then ... the evolution of consciousness becomes the gateway to the wisdom that drives the entire enterprise."

11

Gateway to Wisdom
—Needing God's Presence

Mysterious Spirit-Power,
ultimate force field that generates
the creativity of the cosmos,
we seem to feel your benign presence
behind all that is and is evolving around us.
In the sun and its light,
in the orange-bright morning and the promise of time,
in all that moves and lives,
especially in human caringness and love.
We hear evolutionary music beneath it all.
We revere the thousands of wonders around us
including even the baffling awesomeness of evil
and ignorance
believing that goodness and vitality
have far more potential and sway.
Be with our consciousness this day, Holy God,
persuading us to joy,
to belief that we may live out the full potential
for revelation in every hour.
So be it.

An evolutionary faith constantly makes new demands on us. We once imagined ourselves simply as individuals finding our spiritual way forward, or as members of a family or human circle, walking together as a faith community. The new requirement is to see ourselves not only as part of our earthly bio-region but as part of the entire earth, and even as citizens of the universe.

"We need to become members not only of a locale and not only of the human community," says Thomas Berry. "We need to become members of that wonderful community of all the living and nonliving beings of the world about us. There is no human community in any manner separate from the larger community that surrounds us and on which we are totally dependent for our very breath."

O'Murchu adds: "As a planetary, cosmic species, we belong to a reality greater than ourselves. It is our congruence with our planetary identity and our cosmic potential that bestows genuine power upon us.... As long as we continue to set ourselves against or above the creation in which we are embedded ..., we set ourselves at enmity with the creation to which we belong."

12

Never at Enmity
—When Full of Energy

Eternal Spirit,
may we become all that we were meant to be,
blessed by a consciousness of your presence
and your concerns,
and in harmony with the earth
and its entire living family of creatures.
May we never find ourselves at enmity
with the creation to which we belong,
never insensitive to the injuries
done to our generous earth,
or isolated from human pain and anguish,
finding our personal meaning also
in collective cosmic goals:
complexification and diversity, cooperation, communion.
Give us energy for the demands of life
from your infinite store, Holy One,
from your own spiritual ocean of compassion
and intelligence.
Amen.

A matrix is a kind of web gathered around a center, held together in some organic way. A mother's womb is a matrix with the human embryo at its center. Everything around it keeps it alive. Similarly, each creature in the universe is part of a matrix wherein each element contributes to the life process of the whole.

O'Murchu states that "It is in the survival and thriving of the relational matrix that every aspect of life realizes its full potential and truly becomes itself." Einstein calls it delusory to think of one's self as separated from the rest of reality—a delusion we are all familiar with whenever we hear of or observe someone we consider "other," not acceptable, essentially an outsider, a pariah, untouchable.

Meditation and prayer can be healthy exercises and antidotes to any kind of small-minded thinking. The more alienated people may seem, the more necessary it is—in evolutionary perspective—to stay connected to them somehow. This has always been the instinct of prophetic people, and a part of any deep evolutionary spirituality.

13   *Holy Creating Energy*
—When Needing Community

Holy Creating Energy
in whom we exist
and have our being in all its dimensions,
you have created us in a relational matrix,
a web, a womb,
where everything is connected to everything else,
an existential milieu
that thrives on co-creativity and relationship.
We want to achieve what you would have us to be.
We would evolve and become ourselves
to the full extent of your vision for us.
Come, Evolutionary Spirit,
speak to us in your creation,
fill the hearts of your creatures with large desires,
and kindle in us the fire of your own unfolding dreams.
So be it.

Modern-day physics can be bewildering. Space, it turns out—the concept of a great emptiness—does not really exist at all. For the emptiness we imagine out there is not empty: it is filled with energy, vibration, design—"music," in effect, on both cosmic and microcosmic scales.

In an old song, we sing, "The hills are alive with the sound of music," but that is more than poetic imagining. It is literally true. The world and space are all filled in—filled with vibration, rhythm, and waves. This is also mentioned often in O'Murchu, who writes, "Energy ... is a given reality, apparently with unlimited resourcefulness, and in the unfolding of evolution's great story it exudes as a subtle, vibrational force giving shape and direction to all being and becoming." We are surrounded by many kinds of musical energy. The least we can do is hum along.

14   *God Beyond Us*
—*Broadening Acceptance*

God beyond us, Evolutionary Mystery,
sages in the ancient past have discerned in you
a kind of dancing divinity
to celebrate an indefinable and supreme divine liveliness.
Today scientists imagine your microcosmic world
as made up of a vibrational force
that gives shape to all physical reality.
We rejoice in each dancing strand of energy and music,
and for all prophetic theology casting metaphors of light
on your holy face.
Whatever you are, Spirit God,
we give you reverence and worship.
To do so seems an important part of our peculiar role
in this magnificently mysterious drama.
May it be so.

We take consciousness for granted. After all, we cannot imagine ourselves without it. But in the world around us are many things that are obviously not conscious of themselves. Looking back several million years, we eventually come to an age when nothing at all was conscious: our planet hadn't evolved to that stage. We—our human selves—then, are a recent development, something new in a world finally conscious of itself. We may call ourselves, as O'Murchu does, "evolution growing into a new quality of self-awareness."

Will there be future wonders produced by evolution? Theologian John Haught states that "there is no good reason to think that the general laws of nature have now been suspended. Natural selection will continue to work with remorseless consistency." So as wonderfully as we are made, surely many more wonders lie ahead for this universe.

15

Our Personal Story
—When Grateful for Life

Where does our personal story begin, Holy God of All?
Could it have begun when supernovas expelled carbon
into the open spaces of the universe,
back in history billions of years?
Is that who we are,
participating members of that vast stream of energies
that connect in the gigantic web of our real cosmos?
Is our personal consciousness a meaningful element
in that drama,
the very universe becoming self-conscious?
"How wonderfully and cleverly are we made:
only a little less than the angels," said the psalmist.
With that gift of consciousness, we do give thanks,
lost in wonder.
Amen.

Faced with bafflement, the usual human response is to figure things out as best we can at the moment. For example, we often wonder why people of different cultures act the bewildering way they do. Or we may theorize with colleagues about the apparent randomness of luck and talent.

Questions like these have no answers, of course. We must live with the mystery of it all, even when we don't begin to understand. O'Murchu's synthesis of science and spirit recommends "that we learn to live with mystery and that we develop the wisdom and skill to befriend paradox." It is a mysterious world, but the only one we have.

Scientist Stephen Hawking admits his own mystification: "Although science may solve the problem of how the universe began, it cannot answer the question: Why does the universe bother to exist? I don't know the answer to that."

Science is baffled. Some spiritualities say the universe exists "because God is good and goodness is always outgoing, relational, and expansive." Here the path becomes one of choice, not knowledge.

16   *Imperfect World*
—Feeling Honored to Exist

How can we make sense
of a world of so much imperfection,
Holy Mystery, Evolutionary God?
Is there "a balm in Gilead" to heal our mystification,
an oasis of meaning
amid the desert sands of absurdity and heartache?
A shaft of light, of enlightenment,
emerges from the evidence of a cosmos-wide
evolutionary process
wherein trial and error,
randomness and improvisation, are the very way
of divine creativity.
Open our hearts to hear this news
if there is guidance for us here.
Your creation, God of Light,
is not so much a battleground
as some myths would have it,
or a testing place of good against evil,
or of nation against nation.
It is fundamentally a colossal flower opening up,
a single family tree blossoming and growing,
a cosmic symphony unfolding into meaning and elegance,
where variation and dissonance are necessary
to our evolving process.
This is your beloved world, Enlivening Spirit,
and it is an honor to be an imperfect part of it.
Amen.

To advance ourselves to an evolutionary way of thinking, a shift is necessary for all who have been influenced by the Judeo-Christian tradition: away from imagining ourselves defiled from infancy with a so-called Original Sin. Every child—in an evolutionary world—is a blessing, is thoroughly good and a wondrous new invention, just the way we ourselves instinctively look at infant children. O'Murchu puts it this way: "The perceptual shift—perhaps the first step in the conversion process—is to understand our universe in terms of blessing rather than of curse."

The familiar biblical narrative also suggests to us that God is exterior and located in the heavens above. Almost instinctively in prayer we turn our faces upward, look toward the sky, and beg for a downward suffusion of enlightenment or strength. But *Evolutionary Faith* reminds us that "divine inspiring energy does not emanate from some external heavenly realm, but from within the depths of the creative process itself. The creative energy is an unambiguously inspirited and inspiring life-force."

In other words, we find the spirit of God everywhere and can speak to it and pray to it there—if we have situated ourselves firmly within the evolutionary story and realize the presence everywhere of a God alive and available. If evolution happened and is happening, then God—the spirit mother of life, the spirit father of creation, the Loving Mystery behind and within everything—is at work in it, around us, near us, within us.

17

Most Ourselves
—For Times of Contentment

Eternal Spirit, our parenting creator,
we are most ourselves when we live
with an inner spirit like yours:
extravagant, gratuitous, and innovative.
There seems no better reason for our life and existence
than to be instruments of your outgoing love
and creativity.
We are each chosen,
raised into being by an act of divine goodness
and lavishness.
Give your creatures also that same attitude if you can.
We would make your spirit our own:
generous and inventive.
No spirituality could have a higher aim.
So be it.

How does one learn to grasp what is happening in one's life? Do the episodes of your day mean anything?

Some events are obviously random, chance events without consequence. But overall—once you see your life as a part of a unique evolutionary trajectory, a continuing story that has never happened before—life has meaning, though we may not discern it with any certainty.

In some baffling circumstance, we may find ourselves inquiring of God, "What is the meaning of this?" but without expecting to ever hear an answer or figure it out. "We live in a unique evolutionary moment," says O'Murchu, "and we urgently need to discern the meaning of what is unfolding within and around us." But it is seldom possible to do so satisfactorily. We walk on in mystery, hoping for the best.

18

This Creative Day
—When Giving Thanks

Strong, evolutionary God,
we bless you for this creative day,
for all the novelty and variation
that surrounds each moment
with possibility and hope.
We bless you for the life we have.
We bless you for energy and intelligence,
especially the energies of love and inventiveness.
We bless you for the future,
for each self-reproducing molecule in our bodies
that sweetly carries from one generation to the next
the instructions for the design of future living things
linked to us
and encompassed in our love.
We desire today to be instruments
of your open-ended dreams.
May it be so.

A well-designed automobile can be genuinely awesome. In its elegance we detect—and pay for—the cleverness and wisdom of its designer. Yet, the automobile is not alive; it cannot reproduce itself or evolve into a more "adaptable" model. To achieve that level of artistry would require a greater wisdom in its designer.

That's why we are so in awe of living things and their innate "wisdom," which we call "life." Their elegance is many times greater than that of any self-moving machine or contrivance for flying. Plain "life" is the holiest, most awesome, most elegant thing we will ever encounter. The author of *Evolutionary Faith* puts it this way: "In contemplation … we become receptive … and begin to comprehend the wisdom that is innate to all living things." Einstein felt the same way: "There are only two ways to live your life," he said. "One is as though nothing is a miracle. The other is as if everything is."

19

An Innate Wisdom
—Seeking Enlightenment

Creative Presence, our God,
we would be—with your help—wiser than we are.
We would observe always what we glimpse occasionally:
the wisdom incarnate in all living things,
the harmonies and dissonances within cosmic symphony.
The moving, breathing world of creatures
alive and living around us
is full of astonishing feats of intelligence,
wonderful patterns and structures of cells and organs
that speak continually of your limitless divine life
and confidence in us,
confidence we will find the way
toward living perceptively.
Guide us on the way of faith—and wisdom.
Amen.

The essence of biological evolution is cumulative changes in animal form over time followed by "natural selection": the most adaptable animal survives. Its movement and unfolding is continuous and random, but not automatic. Process theologians expand this concept to include an evolutionary unfolding that began with the Big Bang, a primordial explosion of creativity and energy at the beginning of time and space.

Theists believe that all this force is divine in some way, invented and supported by a spirit we may call "God." According to O'Murchu: "Spiritpower is the driving force of the evolutionary process, the deep secret to unraveling the evolutionary story."

No one can really begin to explain exactly how evolution came about or how it works today, but evidence shows that the evolutionary process is continuing. However, in the thirteenth century Thomas Aquinas also provided logical speculations about how the world worked; yet, he himself wondered if reality was, beneath it all, *totaliter aliter*—entirely otherwise. That could be true of evolution as well, that life and the cosmos are far more elegant and wonderful than we have imagined.

20 A Force We May Trust
—On an Empty Day

Holy Mystery, overflowing with energy,
when life seems repetitious and humdrum,
with empty day sometimes following empty day,
we offer thanks for the very possibility of you,
an all-embracing Spirit-Power and force
behind an evolutionary process,
a Presence to whom we may turn,
a Force we may trust in.
Are we connected with you, Mothering Spirit,
and your melodic dance of infinite possibility,
grounded in the inexhaustible love
of your embracing spirit?
That seems to be true.
Perhaps all our hopes to understand will come to flower
in some way far beyond the reach of our imagination.
May it be so.

11
Prayers of Questioning

I have grave doubts that the story of evolution can be reduced to one cycle, commencing about twelve billion years ago and culminating some five to ten billion years from now. It's all too neat for the creativity of divine becoming.

—Diarmuid O'Murchu

The important thing is not to stop questioning. Curiosity has its own reason for existing.

—Albert Einstein

Holy Spirit of Evolution,
    creator of the cosmos and its wonders,
    how shall we deal with the insidious evil
    —epidemic in world cultures and societies—
    of human egotism,
    cruel in its delusional ignorance
    and destructive of human life and its environment?
Egotism produces war, crime, cruelty,
    disappointment, isolation,
    impoverishment, ignorance, illusion:
    we are all too familiar with these.
In the end, along with all spiritualities of the world,
    we must trust you, Silent Mystery,
    and your evolutionary plan for us
    unfolding at every moment.
We will come together in our pain,
    to pool our wisdom and our energies of hope,
    convinced that in the end, the very end,
    all shall somehow be well.
May it be so.

Where evil comes from—with all its resulting failure and heartbreak—is not something we can understand. Some of it arises from human choice, some comes from the natural evolutionary way of things, but most seems beyond human comprehension. Our hearts cry out for reasons; we seldom find them. Some kind of surrender is called for in every spirituality. O'Murchu speaks of "God's mysterious but wise plan." There is certainly solid evidence of order beneath whatever chaos we may encounter. "God is subtle but not malicious," in Albert Einstein's memorable phrase. However, string theory and quantum mechanics now postulate a pervasive uncertainty beneath any orderliness. There seems to be mystery at every level of reality.

Ultimately, we have no choice but to trust in the world around us, in the marvelous processes of nature that we observe daily, in the forces of healing at work in our bodies and in the earth's apparent ability to govern itself and even heal its wounds, in the ingenuity and heroism of our own human companions. Mystics by and large have been optimists. They lead the way.

Our Overawed Hearts
—At Times of Wordlessness

22

What lies beneath life's unknowns?
We are drawn into your mystery, Holy God,
  wherever we look.
We are awed when we hear
  that the landscape beneath the reach of our microscopes
  may be suffused with tiny strings
  whose vibrational configuration seems to orchestrate
  the evolution of the cosmos
  and undergird all cosmic energies.
All this elegance and music
  has escaped us until modern times.
  What other wonders await?
  In your holy presence we are wordless,
  unable to cope any other way
  with the world before our eyes.
We speak to you in this silence.
You are our God:
  hear the continuing appreciation and worship
  in our overawed hearts.
May it be so.

We may not look into the microscopic world ourselves, but those who do tell stories—like astronauts returning to earth—that amaze us. The most powerful microscopes, which penetrate deep inside the atoms that make up everything, suggest the need to postulate unbelievably tiny but complex strings that vibrate the way a violin string might vibrate as it emits its soaring voice. So we may speculate that a kind of fundamental and harmonious music lies deep in the essence of everything.

When we feel like harmonizing with the world we live in, when we meditate and pray, we well may find ourselves inclined to sway, to hum, to dance, perhaps in a circle or group. That's the kind of world we are part of: a world of communal vibration, novel and unfamiliar as it may seem, though commonplace among primitive peoples. We may have been taught that earth is not our true home, that we do not in fact belong here. This attitude leads to neglect of the earthly environment and to biological disaster.

On the contrary, with the help of modern physics, we find a natural harmony between the submicroscopic makeup of things and our communal and relational instincts: music, rhythm, pulsing movement all carry out the same kind of theme. For O'Murchu, "musical metaphors take on a startling reality, for the theory suggests that the microscopic landscape is suffused with tiny strings whose vibrational patterns orchestrate the evolution of the cosmos."

Utterly Mysterious
—When Feeling Lost

23

How utterly mysterious, Creator Spirit,
   is this existence you have placed us in.
If we were to despair of understanding it at all,
   we could feel justified:
   conflict and tragedy, pain and death surround us
   but so does every kind of love,
   with beauty and wisdom
   in the makeup of every tree and star.
   Astonishing evolutionary forces are measurably at work,
   and there is evidence of genuine altruism among humans.
In addition, we find
   your own mysterious ways gracious and surprising.
Be with us in making sense of it all,
   in keeping up our trust—against so many countersigns—
   that beneath everything is meaning, direction, and promise.
Amen.

The news is seldom good. Death and disappointment and pain and tragedy are part of everyday human life, and we are expected to live with them. They are perhaps the dark side of the evolution that involves us and brings about the future. We have to teach ourselves to accept them and—in an evolutionary view—to even befriend them as we might uncongenial neighbors who will always be there, a familiar part of the world we live in.

Compassion is the capacity to feel what another feels. Altruism is caring unselfishly about others. These qualities are found in heroic women and men, but all of us can reach in that direction. "Our task," said Albert Einstein, "must be ... widening our circle of compassion to embrace all living creatures and the whole of nature in its beauty." It is a task that helps us make sense of this baffling life.

Compassion works best when drawn by the future, when we give our donation to the needy, say, imagining the future joy it will bring about, the good aromatic warm tastes in the mouth; the relief of soul when a conscientious citizen pays a bill; the sweet serenity when long-endured stress is finally gone. This is probably why God feels compassion for us all, because in political exploitation or economic injustice or especially in global degradation, our future is being foreshortened, our colossal promise destroyed. But that's the way evolution "works," drawn by the allure of the future, by survival, by invention, by imagined beauty and expectation of joy. So human compassion should always be identified as an evolutionary feeling, and all compassionate behavior as essentially irreversible creative action.

Loved and Lucky
—Full of Gratitude

24

Some say, Holy God, you are not an entity within this world
    nor an entity outside it and above it,
    that you are instead a reality even deeper
    and less imaginable:
    something like the meaning of it all.
You are within and beneath everything, then,
    as meaning is within and beneath each word
    in human languages.
The energies and persons and events you create
    are, perhaps, words in your own creative language:
    we thank you for them,
    and pray to have the gift of understanding their meaning:
    in their surprise, extravagance, and gratuitousness,
    Mystery Spirit,
    we know we are loved and lucky,
    and give thanks.
Amen.

For many people the word *God* is the supreme puzzle. Some claim that if we think deeply about it, we will see that God is the only true, full being, and everything else is something less. (Philosopher Etienne Gilson described everything else as *pseudo-nonbeings*.) By contrast, others say God is not a being at all, that we cannot really think the thought that is "God," claiming it's empty and misleading. The Buddha warned that asking questions about God would only make us miserable.

Most of us fall somewhere in between: confused. Philosopher Peter Hodgson explains it all this way: "God is ... the being by which beings are. God is the event of world un-concealment by which new meaning and new possibilities of being are created." That is not very clear. What is clear, however, is that all human convictions about God are probably more ambiguous than true, and all our hesitations justified. Obviously, if there is a God, God does not consider clear self-disclosure very important.

What, then, is the use of "prayers" that constantly address "God"? Because prayer creates an avenue—though not the only one—through mystery. It is a poetic discourse some may find congenial, a metaphorical thought style that goes from the known to the unknown, from instinct to action. The human race seems to have found such prayer helpful for many thousands of years.

The Unfolding Process
—Surrendering to God

25

Holy Creative Presence,
we accept the unfolding process of evolution today,
    and we surrender to your mystifying creative dream,
    glistening with divine elegance.
Around us the diversity is bewildering,
    the dangers daunting, the parameters all unknown.
Therefore awe is our silent song,
    and we enter this continuing story with trust,
    accepting your ways as they contrast and school our own.
You are divine, we are your creatures:
    may your creative designs blossom
    and shine in all their beauty and wonder,
    and ourselves be useful in the evolving drama,
    honored to be a part of it.
May it be so.

Scientists argue about the meaning of *intelligent design* and whether one can say it is detectable in complex living things or in the physical world. *Design* may be imprecise, but *elegance* in the world—particularly in the microcosmic world—is undeniable.

For instance, language almost fails us when we attempt to characterize in words the famous double helix that has been found to be the structure at the heart of DNA. But one word certainly applies: *elegance.* Is it *intelligent elegance?* One could say that. O'Murchu writes, "The evolutionary story glistens with divine elegance. Transcendence is written all over it, even in its darkest hours. Unceasingly it points to the grandeur and intimacy of the divine."

What matters is that we walk the world in reverence. Historians of religion have admired the deep veneration of "beauty" in some Native American spiritual chants, a sacred beauty that surrounds each person, each environment, each life. It is a contemplative concept of great value.

Your Joy
—When Pursuing Wisdom

26

Creator of every kind of paradox and puzzle,
Evolutionary Spirit,
    our mystification must be your joy.
    Why else would you hide yourself so effectively?
Do take us gently toward the light.
    Persuade us to learn wisdom
    from the alive and eloquent universe.
Our prayers and philosophizing
    will guide us gradually through the darkness
    and help us sense your holy presence,
    and learn which convictions of ours are promising,
    and which are illusory.
In awe we know your heart,
    and admire your astounding generosity.
    You are our God, the God with us and beyond us.
    We hope to be your joy.
So be it.

It is a theory accepted today by many astronomers that atoms residing right now within our hands and feet and body were forged in the depth of distant stars. They claim that we are all literally made of star dust.

So if we were somehow able to trace to its origin each of the atoms of our body, we would have to point everywhere at once to identify the cosmic matrices from which we have come. In the tens of thousands of stars in the midnight sky, we can see the uncountable sources of our very own life and bodily self.

And if those dreamers are correct who think the cosmos itself may be alive and intelligent, we are not just the dust of the stars: we are their children, their progeny, possibly even their hope and joy.

O'Murchu states the touching mystery this way: "[We are] begotten from within the womb of an alive universe." That alive universe may be unimaginable to us but is not, for that reason, an impossibility.

Please Create Them
—Dreaming Great Dreams

27

Holy Source of all,
it is suggested by scientists that wherever there is light,
    there is life,
    that light and heat are mysteriously life-producing.
Others add that life naturally evolves
    toward affectivity and intelligence.
    Such a possibility helps make sense of our universe.
    Were it true, then exciting worlds of life
    might surround us out in the distant reaches of space,
    linked to us in a cosmic web of light.
If stars and galaxies
    are made of the same substances as is our earth,
    aren't they necessarily also made, like ours,
    of evolving intelligences and persons?
Do those minds in outer space wonder about us,
    as we do about them?
    Have we even somehow a common destiny,
    some great in-gathering at the end of it all,
    an encounter and communion of personalized spirits
    from every corner of the universe?
Our human longing is that such cosmic companions do exist,
    and if they do not,
    then, limitlessly imaginative Spirit-Womb of us all,
    please create them.
Amen.

O'Murchu believes there is value in theological speculation that leads to prayer. He says, "To move from speculation to trust, we need to move from human certainty to cosmic confidence." Certainty is precious in this world, but a rare achievement. Often we say, "I feel certain that ..." something is true when we really are banking on trust, not certainty. We often just trust our gut instincts and have no other choice.

Especially when it comes to human love and friendship, there is never anything better than trust and instinct. Scientific certitude is not a concept applicable to a discussion of personal relationships—or religion and spirituality, for that matter. You have to rely on something like instinct.

Thus it is foolish to attempt to arrive at some kind of scientific certitude in tracing the provable fingerprints of God in the world around us. It is enough that we find creation awesome. Awe—that hard-to-define but frequent human experience—is the very beginning point of prayer and spirituality. Heroes are born only under the influence of awe. "I'd die for you" is an expression of devotion—and awe. Yet awe is immeasurable, almost undefinable, and doubtlessly unscientific. The "cosmic confidence" O'Murchu speaks of is built on much less provable stuff.

Unimaginable God
—Baffled by the Mysterious

28

We cannot begin to imagine you, Holy Mystery,
  prodigiously alive and creative.
When human religions try to get a supreme being
  into an image or an icon,
    they often end up with the grotesque:
    thousands of eyes, dozens of healing hands,
    mountain ranges of potency.
How can there exist beneath all that is a creating spirit
  who invents and produces this elegant cosmos,
  who gives it its freedom and wild possibilities,
  who asks its companioning persons
  and co-creators—ourselves—
  to surrender to so many unthinkable threats and sufferings,
  and finally to accept death and the unknown?
Is a "god" thinkable?
Yet you, Unknown Spirit, must exist in some way:
  the streaming reality evolving around us demands a source.
We give thanks for questioning moments like this,
  Holy Mystery,
  unimaginable God.
Amen.

One of the problems with believing in the existence of a supreme being is the apparent implausibility of it. Fervent believers often do not help when they suggest they know all about God—"his" name, "his" gender, "his" role (he's "the Lord"), even "his" whereabouts (in the sky).

To begin properly we have to admit all that we don't know. A child given crayons in a religious education class began with passion, and the teacher asked what she was about to draw.

"God," she replied.

"But nobody knows what God looks like," said the adult.

She answered without looking up, "They will soon."

Adults are just as amusing when they claim too much information about God.

On the other hand, many ordinary people admit to a very honest bafflement about the cosmos, asking: How did this reality come about? How is it put together and held together? Scientists, too, ask these very humble questions, as did Einstein, who once wrote: "I want to know how God created this world. I am not interested in this or that phenomenon, in the spectrum of this or that element. I want to know God's thoughts. The rest are details."

Your Gracious Energies
—Bewildered and Fearful

29

We turn our thoughts and hearts to you,
    Mysterious Evolutionary God,
    especially at times of bewilderment.
Is there reason for hope?
Our worldview, patched together
    with fragile elements of intelligence and illusion,
    at times seems to be coming apart.
In your numinous presence, Holy Mystery,
    we realize that total calamity is never going to happen,
    that despair is unjustified: there is a God.
Every dissolution and death
    though facilitated by our own foolishness
    can ultimately be saved by your evolutionary energies
    and become part of a hopeful future all unforeseen by us.
We give thanks then, Creating Spirit,
    for our sovereignty and freedom
    even when, as a race, we use it poorly.
Amen.

Hope is always possible. We live in an environment that seems ultimately benign and friendly to us, making human life congenial and sometimes even ecstatically delightful. And we live in what the evolutionary poet, scientist, and mystic Teilhard de Chardin called "the divine milieu," with God as our context. Our world contains the divine. We can always find spiritual comfort that in some sense—though not scientifically provable—there is a supreme being, though not a God "above," not an all-powerful "Lord," not a deity either female or male. The towering genius Albert Einstein spoke of experiencing a "deeply emotional conviction of the presence of a superior reasoning power." That may be our experience as well.

O'Murchu writes: "We will not resolve the dilemma [of bewilderment] by escapism or denial. We need to reclaim and remember what our lives are meant to be about. We need to reclaim the cosmic and planetary context of our existence." *Context* usually refers to a printed page, calling attention to the importance of where a word or idea is printed, what other ideas are on that page, and what the whole chapter is about. Similarly, humans exist in a *context* that stretches over the entire world and into the sky and universe where the world originated. We are part of it all, and its great story is our story. Its great purpose and glory are our purpose and glory as well.

Deep Understanding
—Deep Questioning

30

As we reach for deep understanding,
  Holy Surrounding-us Sophia, our God,
  we are in awe.
Who are you, God of All?
The wild diversity of life-forms on earth
  is an astonishing manifestation of creative power.
A symphony of invention fills all space,
  all our milieu,
  as it evolves ever new dimensions and shapes,
  breathtaking in its variety and accommodation,
  vitality and wisdom.
Our milieu, this earthen community,
  and its atmosphere and sky,
  is magnificent beyond words:
  and some suspect it may even be itself
  conscious, intelligent, and even personal.
That is almost too wonderful to think:
  yet you, Creator Spirit, are yourself a supreme wonder
  and yet we can believe in you.
We give you our thanks and worship, wholly inadequately
  but with sincerity and trustful openness.
Amen.

Perhaps at one time the scientific study of the earth and sky was academic, taking place mostly at sleepy universities. No more. Now that evolution is widely accepted by the scientific community, studies of earth and sky have exploded into a new revelation of a Creator most present and most elegant, and a creation bursting with vitality and diversity.

"It is time to embrace a universe exuding vitality and wisdom," states author Diarmuid O'Murchu, "consciously manifesting its innate power in variety and diversity of all life-forms, our home planet being the connective tissue that links our human intelligence with the cosmic wisdom that endows the whole of creation." In evolutionary spirituality, the future St. Francis will sing not only of Brother Sun and Sister Moon, but of Brother Chance and Sister Chaos, Cousin Surprise and Uncle Randomness.

God of Closeness
—Doubting Everything

31

Holy Cloud of Being,
   God of radical and intimate closeness,
   in your presence we pray our inadequate words
   of adoration and surrender.
You have blessed us with life and consciousness,
   with mobility and creativity:
   we would, for our part, fulfill all your intentions for us
   though every thought we have of you
     is paradoxical and inadequate.
Are you *one?*
Are you *intelligent?*
Are you *loving?*
   We reply to each question: Yes,
   but in almost no way we normally conceive of those terms.
Holy, Unknown Being,
   you are everything to us.
Amen.

GOD OF CLOSENESS

Once we see that the Divine Mystery, God, is not an easy, mind-friendly entity but rather a paradoxical, almost contradictory *being,* then we can grasp how we need new metaphors to take us from what we know to what we don't know. At that point, thinking of God as something like a good mother or a generous father or another loved one can be helpful. We let our experience carry us beyond experience: along the path of poetry. O'Murchu expresses it this way: "When we encounter the evolutionary story, we encounter the big God at the heart of it all, but also the God of radical, intimate closeness, energizing, befriending, empowering, and affirming us at every stage of the way, truly, the image of the birthing and nurturing mother."

Darwin himself continued to speak of a "Creator" to the end of his life, though he seems to have been a kind of "reluctant agnostic," says theologian John Haught. In whatever way we may classify our spirituality at the moment, it makes sense to remain open to other expressions and figures of speech. We are in the arena of deepest mystery, and no one can say where further thought and experience may take us.

Mystery Beyond Us
—When God Is Distant

32

Holy Life-Force, God of this unfolding world,
Mystery beyond us, Loving Wisdom,
   all the efforts of our imagination
   to catch you and name you
   ultimately fail.
You are beyond us
   because you are beyond all concepts
   and clarifying metaphors.
We cannot really embrace you,
   but know that you in effect embrace us
   and hold us in your benign and protective gaze.
Yet you are also not the same as any earthly parent
   or mentor we have known.
You may rejoice, as a loyal sibling might,
   in all we are and do.
   Yet you are also unlike any earthly brother or sister,
   friend or lover.
You are, you exist: that is the heart of our faith and hope.
   We are yours, and all our meaning is in you.
We give thanks.
Amen.

To have a rational and mature spirituality, we need to question who we might be in God's eyes, how we appear to the mind of the Great Mind. Then we will discover—to put the answer succinctly—we are beautiful, we are elegant, we are beloved.

God's embrace of us is infinitely benign, and irrevocably so. That transcendent caringness all around us and within us is permanent and all-knowing. We can feel washed to absolute authenticity in that divine gaze, which sees us totally, loving us exactly as we are. As O'Murchu puts it: "We begin … to comprehend the wisdom that is innate to all living things, the creation that is endowed with a potential for meaning and self-becoming. We realize once more that everything is held—and held irrevocably—in the embrace of a benign life-force."

What of our pain? What of our heartbreak? What of failure and hatred and death? There is no answer that works except faith, faith that as dawn defeats night and spring defeats winter, the unfolding forces of a loving evolutionary God, the God of Justice still, can and will renew somehow—we know not how—all that is lost along the way.

—At Times of Self-Doubt

Thank you, God of All,
    co-creator of our world,
    for allowing us to be imperfectly made—
    because it makes us, if we are wise, forgiving.
Do you accept us as we are?
    We condemn people too quickly:
    we judge them for flawed thinking, disguised egotism,
    unworthy acquisitiveness, or skewed opinions.
But we can forgive them once we accept our own shadow,
    and realize how well we ourselves fit
    into the ranks of a less than perfect human race.
You, Holy God, accept each of us,
    prophets tell us, *just as we are*—
    provided our moral judgments of others
    are reciprocally generous and compassionate.
Imperfection fits this evolving reality,
    for the universe thrives on diversity,
    including random failure,
    one of the very preconditions for the unfolding advances.
May it be so.

The orthodox Christian view of the world is that our reality is somehow deeply flawed, that, in fact, every human being is deeply flawed too—the result of Adam's sin—all of us now with darkened minds and weakened wills. Therefore, we should not expect too much of human beings; we all need the sacraments of priests to give us the strength to survive spiritually.

Some theologians in ancient times went so far as to claim that simply being female, for instance, was itself a creational flaw and produced weakness and an inclination to dishonesty and disobedience. That is, in fact, the subtle suggestion of the Book of Genesis, the first book of the Bible. But O'Murchu's synthesis of evolution and faith stands against all this unjustified negativity: "[The creation] may look flawed to us humans, but there is little to suggest that it is flawed in the eyes of that deeper wisdom that keeps the whole thing in being."

Too Much Magnetism
—When Love Prevails

34

Your creation, Holy God, is at times elegant beyond belief.
　You have somehow laced the world
　　with too much magnetism.
Not only are polarized metals drawn to each other
　and not only do massive whirling planets cling together
　　across the vastness of separating space;
　even stinkbugs feel drawn inexorably to stinkbug mates,
　and zebras to zebras, and humans to humans,
　often caring and joyful
　beyond any reproductive possibilities,
　sometimes beyond any purpose
　other than the pleasure of love,
　even against ironclad customs of culture,
　or the mortal anger of a threatened ideology.
Is not all this magnetism the engine of our creative unfolding?
　But there's too much of it, Holy Spirit!
　We find it impossible to control, and hard to understand:
　it's frightening, numinous.
We watch in awe as love prevails
　when so much stands against it.
　For all these wonders, we give you awed thanks.
Amen.

We are our links to others, in a sense. Each of us may say: I was literally inconceivable without two people getting together, linked in physical relationship. Then, sparked into being, I was linked to a mother for nine months, then caught up into a weblike circle of people, all connected in some way to each individual and to the whole. In fact, everything I gradually became through education and experience was built on relationships to others, to knowledge held in common, and to communal experiences of many kinds.

Civil laws must be updated when they oppose caring and harmless relationships among people. O'Murchu refers to this when he speaks of "Jesus inviting disciples to a new way of relating beyond the dominant and oppressive structures of his day." Nothing is more evolutionary than human love and magnetism.

So Dark a Mystery
—In God's Absence

35

So dark is your mystery, Holy God,
   that we must enter the world of the absurd to find you.
   Your existence indeed seems an absurd belief
   in a world of such pain, randomness, and injustice,
   but your nonexistence would be arguably even more so.
Along any path of cautious inquiry,
   we see before us an evolving cosmos blazing in elegance,
   astonishingly orderly and fixed,
   scientifically predictable in its numerous constants,
   one phenomenon more astonishing than the next:
      magnetism, gravity, light,
      then living things, then consciousness.
Evolutionary evidences overwhelm us
   and even overwhelm judicious skepticism.
   Do they not point to powerful forces at work
   organized by a caring intelligence?
You have almost escaped us, Elusive Mystery,
   but still we find you in the darkness
   and honor your luminous unknowability.
Amen.

According to contemporary Buddhist teacher Thich Nhat Hanh: "Discussing 'God' is not the best use of our energy." Still, the discussion is inevitable. Hanh would admit that, of course, but would not expect the discussion to be satisfactory. The real trouble is that often our "God/ess" is not "big, elastic and embracing enough"—in the phrase of theologian Mary Hunt. We often have preconceived concepts of the divine that limit the discussion. We still imagine God as distant, as above us in the sky, obsolete though as that notion is.

A familiar suggestion is that the musicians and composers are the mystics and prophets of today. They dream up the sound architecture that transubstantiates the mysterious into the audible, an audible that suggests there is a meaning and beauty beyond perfect order and the rational. One could say it is they who most appropriately are translating the real nature of things into understandable, comprehensible analogs, audible metaphors beyond the conceptual ones we are used to in literature.

Without analogs, the divine mystery escapes us completely, an experience that surely was meant to happen that way.

Make Us Lovers
—When Knowing Love

36

Are you, Eternal Spirit, full of erotic energy?
  Can we trace our own drive for relationality back to you?
  Is not that heartfelt magnetism among lovers
    your own numinous paradigm?
  Does it speak of you, model you, reveal you?
  It seems to.
You are a God of Love, then—above all other identities.
  Love is your premier creation.
It is lovers who are your first mystics,
  and it is lovers who should guide the world
  in almost every way,
  lead the religions, lead the nations, and lead the leaders.
Make us lovers, then, God of Love.
  Fill us with your own spirit.
May it be so.

The *erotic* may sound to us like something debased and carnal. That is regrettable because erotic feelings are above all a creation of God and a revelation of what our world is all about.

In fact, according to O'Murchu, *erotic* is not too strong a word to apply to the divine spirit itself, and to all the healthy energies essential to the evolution of the world. The Big Bang also can be thought of as erotic, an unimaginable outburst of love and creativity. In *Evolutionary Faith*, O'Murchu states: "If we take seriously the creative Spirit at the heart of the evolutionary process, then we must spare no effort to attune ourselves with the Spirit's wild, erotic energy."

Our sexual experiences might consequently be seen as potentially religious, as revelatory, as sacred. We might express gratitude in symbol, like candlelight, or gesture, like the instinctive motion of hand to heart. All our human love experiences have the potential to take us into the world of the sacred, and in that light the debasement of them is sacrilege.

Conscious Communion
—When Wisdom Is Our Ideal

37

Holy Ocean of Creativity around us and within us,
   can you give us open eyes and minds
   so that we do not find ourselves at war
   with the creation to which we belong?
If we are aware of the crucial clue
   —that everything is linked to everything else—
   we can live more relationally,
   more connected to our environment and our community,
   in more conscious communion with the earth
   and with those we love and encounter.
You are the eternal Spirit:
   give us all a more comprehensive perspective
   that enables us to live larger lives
   and cherish ever-larger hopes.
Amen.

Humanlike animals have walked the earth for some four million years, according to anthropologists. Our own specific human species goes back at least twenty-five thousand years with clear evidence of other human species before that, often simultaneously.

It would be tragic if all that elegant development were condemned to extinction and suffocation because of the climate changes brought about mostly by our human overuse of oil. Heroic efforts now can supposedly save us—but few humans are hearing the alarm.

Our own nation is especially deaf to the warnings, while most other nations on earth are taking courageous steps to help. The United States could make the difference, but our approach to international affairs does not auger well for cooperation among nations. Instead, human greed and arrogance could eventually precipitate the end of all life on earth.

O'Murchu underlines this threat. "As long as we continue to set ourselves against or above this creation ..., all that we will achieve is more sickness, pain, alienation and meaninglessness. We set ourselves at enmity with the creation to which we belong. Ironically, we may be paving the pathways of our own destruction." An evolutionary faith and spirituality could strengthen us to do and promote what is necessary for the earth's survival as a human habitat.

Immediate Listener
—Knowing God's Intimacy

38

Are you the *deity* some refer to, God of Evolution,
  Holy Sophia, Wise Mothering Spirit?
Deity carries the feeling of distance, remoteness,
  and the theoretical,
    but we know you as a lively and immediate listener,
    a compassionate, caring companion,
    the underlying source of all energy
    and intelligence in the universe.
Even your loving face is not very far out of range:
    perhaps only as far as death,
    or reflected in the faces of everyone we meet.
We are looking and listening.
Be there, Relational Liveliness that energizes the universe!
Amen.

According to *Wise Women* by Susan Cahill, the Goddess Sophia is the name given by the Hebrew Scriptures to stress the feminine aspect of the divine mystery, implying the concept of "an ontology of relationship."

In other words, if there is relationship, not singleness, in God, then there is the same in all of God's creatures. Nothing exists that is not connected to everything else.

The name *Sophia* ("Wisdom") reminds us, says Cahill, of the very attractive notion that in the beginning was community. In trinitarian and Christian terms, the name *Sophia* also suggests a God that is not lonely and solitary, but "an otherness of persons within the oneness of God," a relational entity, perhaps no longer Father, Son, and Holy Ghost—but possibly Wisdom, Love, and Intelligence. If this thought—three persons, one God— does not seem "thinkable," at least it reminds us of the need for metaphor in approaching the ultimate mystery, and underlines the unknowability and unnameability of any ultimate divinity.

Divine Communion
—The Grandeur of Justice

39

Holy Wise Divine Communion of Energies,
   Evolutionary God,
      what are you to us?
You are more than the ground of our being:
   you are the ground of what should be
   and what we trust will be.
   You are the ground of justice and of hope.
Thus we discover your graciousness in our hearts,
   supporting our instinct for the unselfish, the fair,
   and the harmonious.
Could it be
   that by growing close to your passionate desires
   for justice and abundant life
   we grow close to you in your essence?
Thank you, Ocean of Mystery,
   for all your surreptitious inspiration.
Amen.

While a Christ or messiah is promised in the ancient Hebrew Scriptures, people persist in hoping that a human, historical messiah will appear on earth and make everything right. Actually, the rabbi Jesus of Nazareth seems to be the most messiahlike person to come along thus far in history— though he fails to rise to the full expectations of the Hebrew Scriptures, establishing justice and peace worldwide. Still, the ideal of worldwide "justice" or fairness is a particularly winning and authenticating theme of the tradition.

Those sacred books, though wonderful in both concept and literary elegance, did not in fact record a real promise that came directly from God, but rather seem to be—according to Rabbi David Sperling and others— invented, using as raw material incidents and personages known to oral tradition. Superbly gifted leaders wrote them down to help build a nation, to give it a "history" and a dream: in effect, a mythology. And it worked. Judaism holds together largely because it honors its stories and rituals. Christianity, seeing itself as a fulfillment of Judaism, considers itself one single "mystical Body of Christ." This ideal seems genuinely evolutionary, since without cooperation civilization cannot proceed toward justice.

But perhaps most helpful today are those theologians who teach that we are on our own as humans, that we must communally be our own "christ" and messiah, must each take responsibility for justice and the sustainability of our world habitat, especially that part of it where we can have an effect. Otherwise, our world will never become a just and humane home for all living creatures on our planet.

God of Light
—In Times of Gratitude

40

Holy God of Light,
    empowering Spirit of wisdom wherever it appears,
    why do we yearn for an ever-brighter perspective,
    more truth and less illusion?
Still we value the beauty of where we stand.
Our song each day is gratitude,
    thankfulness especially for the inspiring people in our lives,
    the wise and prophetic models of a radical relationality,
    a relatedness that makes life lively,
    that fosters creativity and personal evolution.
Give us for this work the devotion of disciples
    in pursuit of communal aims
    along with the sovereignty of self-valuation
    come what may.
  Amen.

Our times call out for networks, for connection, for relationships of humans with humans and with all living things. Isolation and privilege may once have been idealized: the holy hermit, the royal family in their palace, the wealthy landowner-lord, the solitary scholar, the celibate monk. No more. Out of the women's movement, for instance, has come the realization of a "yearning for connection" that Audre Lorde spoke of and exemplified.

Our world is in fact one, and we will all survive or become extinct together. The spiritualities that are most useful today are those that are "relational," that are truly "catholic," that reach out and take in everybody and everything, not those male-defined spiritualities praising a solitary "per-fection" and sainthood for a few. O'Murchu refers to the life of Jesus as "an exemplary model of radical relationality that fosters creativity, equality, and justice," then calls on us to use those virtues "in our guardianship of cre-ation and its evolutionary process." It's a truly contemporary spiritual ideal.

III
Prayers of Ambiguity

Darkness ... often characterizes the spiritual journey.

—Diarmuid O'Murchu

The most beautiful experience we can have is the mysterious.

—Albert Einstein

Language often fails us. For some people, calling God "personal" conveys more ambiguity than truth—for if God is "personal," then "he" is also heartless. No "person" they could imagine would create a world so full of anguish, pain, and absurdity—alongside such colossal beauty and elegance.

Yet, most of those who want to accept the idea of a personal God only mean to credit the creator Spirit with intelligence and caringness. In that sense, we may say that God, the Great Mystery around us, is personal. But perhaps not "a person." God can think, can care; but God is otherwise like no "person" we know of.

Further undesirable ambiguity is introduced when thinking of the divinity as singular, as "one," one God. A sign hanging in Einstein's office at Princeton said, "Not everything that counts can be counted, and not everything that can be counted counts."

The notion of "one" of something means that you are counting, you are imagining something that can conceivably be two or three. But God cannot really be imagined. Yet, even in the Christian doctrine of the Trinity, there is oneness of essence and oneness of existence: it is only in "relationality" that the Trinity is multiple, the medieval theologians claimed.

God escapes both our definition and our description, yet our race seems to have always suspected the existence of an infinite creator Spirit. Today the scientific evidences of an evolutionary, life-unfolding energy beneath, within, and beyond all that is, baffles—and awes—us more than ever.

41

Beyond Us
—When Words Fail

What are you like, Ocean of Mystery, source of all that is:
and should we speak of *"you"* at all?
"You" is the personal pronoun,
and is it not callow to think of your baffling essence as
personal like our own,
as thoughtful, as caring—
and not rather beyond such attributes?
But, like our religious forebears,
we shall try to use human language nevertheless,
advancing in tenuous metaphor
from the known to the unknown.
What is more, are you not also in fact—
if we listen to theologians—
beyond the singleness of any personhood we know of?
May you be more understandable somehow
as a multiple divinity?
Three persons, as the Christians have it?
An infinite number of persons, as the Hindus think?
Holy Divinity beyond us,
we bless you out of our darkness, lost in your mystery.
Amen.

In the minds of people we call mystics, there seems to be a continuing sense that one is always able to cross the bridge to God and to God's mind, and that the Divine Mystery can speak to us somehow, and cares about us, cares infinitely. That mystic sense of God, however, is surrounded by darkness, by a "cloud of unknowing." *The Cloud of Unknowing* is a short book written by an unnamed Christian monk about 1370 c.e., stressing the great distance between provable sense experience and a knowledge of God. It helps us understand how science can seem so un-theistic or even anti-theistic, and conversely how some seekers find the existence of God so obvious: the paths are different. "It was not my rational consciousness," said Einstein, "that brought me to an understanding of the universe."

"Lift up your heart to God," says the author of *The Cloud*, "and mean God's self, and not what you can get out of him." "God's self" is what we seek. The cloud of unknowing is dark but not wholly opaque. In *Evolutionary Faith*, O'Murchu writes: "Darkness ... often characterizes the spiritual journey. Real though that darkness is, it never clouds the foundational relationality that is the core perception and conviction of mystical consciousness."

42

We Ask for Courage
—In Need of Faith

Where is courage to be found, Holy Spirit,
Creator and Inventor of ultimate mystery?
We need it each day
if only because darkness
so often characterizes the spiritual journey.
Even if we hesitantly choose the option
of belief in life's benignity,
still we stand bewildered—for often enough faith only leads
to another level of darkness.
We feel you are present, but are you on our side?
We envy untroubled believers,
but how can they be paying attention?
Daily we have to face ever-new choices
of belief or disbelief,
trust or distrust.
Encourage us, Spirit God, if you can.
Our hearts are restless,
even when our core perception
is of your presence and call.
Help us surrender to the mysteries of the evolving reality.
It seems the only option that makes sense,
ambiguous though it be.
Amen.

The promise of a messiah as savior of the world was a brilliant invention of the ancient Jewish writers. To dedicate oneself to the welfare of others is a healthy human ideal for everyone—and devotees of all the Abrahamic religions are called on to be deeply messianic in their personal lives. Today we know it is not sin that any messiah must save us from, but above all from the catastrophic loss of the entire human habitat.

A recently published article, "This Overheating World," in the British magazine *Granta*, stated that nine of the world's ten warmest years since records have been kept occurred in the past fourteen years.

It goes on. "The world we were born into has gone. We shall never completely recapture its climate, its seasons, the way its plants grew and its animals lived. This is not a wild-eyed warning, a man on the street with a placard 'THE END IS NIGH!' Respectable science knows it and says it.... Some calculations suggest that, as it gets warmer, the average garden in effect moves south, climatically, by a distance of sixty-six feet every day. It's getting warmer everywhere. Who is responsible? We are—our habits. Can we prevent it? Too late. Can we moderate it, slow it, eventually reverse it? Yes—if we try."

So far most efforts to, literally, save the world have been heartbreakingly in vain. But a new consciousness is evolving, and every spirituality can take new hope in its evolution.

43

Holy Fire at the Heart of Mystery,
there are losses in life that break our hearts—
especially if we send out our affections profusely.
Losses come, failure happens,
energy dissipates and is lost,
our efforts all in vain at times.
Be near, Holy Wisdom,
and strengthen our hearts if you can,
but above all enable us to befriend
the perplexing world we have
along with all its imperfection, illusion,
and disappointment.
Persuade our hearts to accept the world as it is
and to work for our planet home's survival.
It is the life you have given us for now,
and in your promising presence
we can walk its paths responsibly and courageously.
Be with us.
Amen.

Pain is felt as an obvious evil, but it is not something invented by God. That would assume the obsolete paradigm of an "almighty God." Rather, pain is often something—given the nature of things—beyond any conceivable control, a part of the native randomness of the way things must be in order to evolve. According to the O'Murchu synthesis of science and spirit: "Things evolve according to principles bigger and deeper than what we humans envisage."

Yet, pain is never totally negative and might even mark a creative moment. Hunger is pain; symptoms and clues of illness are often pain; discomfort alerts us to life's primary needs. If we had no pain experience at all in life, perhaps we would never learn to be compassionate and reach out to those in need. The whole opening of our soul begins in pain, as does our independent human life, starting with the ordeal of childbirth, painful for both mother and child. Even the very procreative conception of a firstborn necessarily begins in hymenal blood.

From beginning to end, life's parameter on all sides is pain. When we've done all we can to alleviate it, then surrender to its evolutionary meaning becomes the only spiritual path we can tread, whether we choose it or not.

44

With Me in Pain
—In Times of Anguish

Are you with us in every pain and anxiety,
Evolutionary Spirit,
Holy God of magnificence beyond our knowing?
For all your majesty and bewildering otherness,
still you are a compassionate and caring creator
for the best human parents and friends
were each your inventions too,
given to this world to be your paradigms, your agents,
your incarnations.
We feel your closeness,
dear Mystery,
in times of anguish, and rejoice nevertheless
in your continuing gift of life and time.
Amen.

Every human being clings to life in a primordial way. It is as instinctual as breathing. Only when life becomes painful and meaningless do we question that instinct. The wise can even make sense of death. O'Murchu writes: "With graced intuition we [are] at ease about the fact that death is a precondition for new life; we do not know why, but it is."

Probing the possibility of life after death does not constitute a scientific inquiry. No one can make a factual statement about it. The idea comes from human desire—so it may simply be wishful thinking—but it also comes from the religions of the world and from philosophers of every age, most of "the best and the brightest."

Some scientists reason that life after death would harmonize with scientific facts—since matter and energy are never destroyed, but only changed. Extinction of matter or energy is not a phenomenon that science has ever witnessed. Further, if we see "justice" as a necessary part of human life and the world's creator as a just God, then—since so many humans experience deep injustice in their human life—there must be another existence where everyone will have a fair chance for joy and success.

But no one knows. Once we have played our evolutionary role and given our energies and talents to further in our small way the greater story taking place around us, we must peacefully leave the future to whatever mysterious—and hopefully benign—outcomes there may be.

45

God of Evolution
—Looking Beyond Despair

God of Evolution, we thank you for both life and death:
for a life that is full of promise,
but also for life's ending,
believing that death, and every surrogate of death
—pain, failure, depression, injury, disappointment—
can be redeemed from its absurdity
because they are, in evolutionary perspective,
preconditions for new life.
The way things work in your world, Holy God—
a world of freedom
and therefore genuine chance, randomness, and danger—
is a kind of Spirit-impelled trajectory toward the future.
Every natural happening
draws us ultimately to fulfillment
as surely as day follows night.
What is required is perspective, a long-term view.
We ask you for that, God of every holy gift.
May it be so.

Is it impossible to see God? Yes, but we can see the work of God, detecting the fingerprints of some amazing holy creator at work. Albert Einstein said, "My religion consists of a humble admiration of the illimitable superior spirit."

Where is that spirit? Most detectably in the flow of energies within our world, according to O'Murchu, citing as his source physicist Eric J. Chaisson. For O'Murchu and Chaisson, energy is the very connective tissue and force of all evolutionary change and growth. Apparently, our own personal energies are part of this phenomenon, a participation in the creative process that we may experience—if we are reflective—every day of our life.

When we are creative—taking time to shape the future, to invent the music that decorates the air around us, to put together a home where human spirits and bodies can grow and relate, learn and find joy and love in life, to carry out our giftedness to its natural fulfillment—it is the energies of evolution, the energies of the Divine Mystery itself, at work in us.

46 *Your Creativity*
—Feeling the Energized God

Holy Spirit-Force,
it is energy that is the most tangible evidence
of your creativity at work in the cosmos,
an energy transforming into the wonder
of an evolving universe,
holding the elements in their order
through the burgeoning chaos,
keeping all the objects in space in gravitational balance
amid innovational unfolding,
an energy beating in uncountable living hearts,
in every mating song,
and in the whole offbeat symphony
that is our living milieu.
We give you our appreciation
and our surrender, Holy God,
with thanksgiving to be alive
and, thankfully, energized.
Amen.

The Great Mystery—whom we may call "God," though the mystery we speak of has no real name—is everywhere, hiding especially in each numinous element of nature, appearing in different cultures and eras as Wind, as Storm, as Magnetic Force, as Life Source, as Love, as Death, as Creative Inventor, as Beauty, as the mothering Earth, as all-caring Sky Father, as Star-Maker.

God may even appear as Destiny. "*Ad Te creasti nos,*" wrote the genius Augustine at the beginning of his *Confessions,* addressing God: "You have made us for yourself." At death we may safely hand ourselves over, surrender ourselves, to the great mystery, greater than our individual selves and our private concerns. We must, O'Murchu says, "embrace the cosmic and planetary context within which our life story and the story of all life unfolds. We belong to a reality greater than ourselves."

"Into your hands I commend my spirit," said the dying prophet Jesus of Nazareth, citing the Hebrew Scriptures he loved and lived by. At the end he entrusted himself "into God's hands," seeing death as a return to his source, an idea that gave meaning to even the most painful and apparently absurd circumstances.

47

We Need Not Know
—Thankful to Be Useful

Our hearts abound in joy, Holy Mystery,
to belong to a reality far greater than ourselves
where we discover the loving face of a benevolent mystery
and within which everything—ourselves included—
is blessed with purpose and meaning.
We need not know what that purpose is
or just how to define our meaning.
We need not be happy with our role.
Still with faith we entrust ourselves
to an evolving cosmos,
and rest in a reality
that is—we believe—full of meaning,
and ultimately good.
Amen.

Who would not enjoy knowing for certain that the central task in one's life will be a success? If we live in an undefined narrative, that kind of confidence is never within reach. But if we make ourselves a part of the story of evolution, of a narrative that involves the entire cosmos, then our smaller successes or failures matter less. The larger story will succeed: it is God's own plan, and we can rejoice in that. O'Murchu suggests: "We need to move from the compulsive need for human certainty to a trust in cosmic hope."

Is that possible? In this age of science and skepticism, is there still support for a life of hope, of faith and spirituality? There is, though faith for us may be mostly reverence—especially reverence for life, Albert Schweitzer's ideal—and spirituality mostly awe. Many of the world's greatest scientists and philosophers find themselves in this place. Einstein himself admitted, "I belong to the ranks of devoutly religious men." "There are only two ways to live your life," he said. "One is as though nothing is a miracle. The other is as if everything is."

48

You Are with Us
—Intuiting God's Presence

We know, Holy Compassionate Mystery,
that your involvement in the evolutionary process is total,
and so, even in the random and chance events
that often bring about so much human pain,
you do not stand aside
but rather are with us in the storm,
urging quietly that we do not lose heart,
that all will be well,
urging that we trust you
and your unfolding plan of love and creativity,
a system larger and more ambitious
than we can begin to imagine
but in which we—in our surrender—are a crucial part.
Be with us in our vital energies
as well as in our devout submission.
Amen.

A homing pigeon knows instinctively that it has a home: where that is and if he can get there remain unanswered questions until he tries. Humans may have a similar homing instinct—and if we can take the myths and literatures of every nation as testimony, that homing instinct seems part of being human. From that instinct comes our common human yearning for a life beyond death. Most religions believe in it.

Some would call all this mere wishful thinking. Others say it's a natural part of us. Without a life beyond death, human existence for many people would be grossly unfair and unjust, even cruel and absurd. With it, life as it is makes better sense, it seems. The O'Murchu synthesis of an evolutionary faith contains the presumption of a life after death. He writes: "God has been at work in evolution right from the beginning. That same prodigiously creative God always is ahead of us in the future," an attitude full of promise.

Christian theologian Paul Tillich claimed: "Being religious means asking passionately the question of the meaning of our existence and being willing to receive answers, even if the answers hurt." Many find it is the questions that are painful, especially when there are no answers at all. We may choose to believe, or to half-believe and half-doubt, or to disbelieve. What matters—and makes for peace—is our tolerance, mutual respect, and openness.

49

Your Gracious Being
—Longing for a Life Without End

Holy God of Mystery,
miracles of love and generosity occur before our eyes:
we take them as sacraments
of your own goodness and mercy.
Heroic people inspire us.
But whatever exists flows somehow
from your mysterious essence.
Because people care, we suspect you care.
Because we can be thoughtful,
we suspect you, our source, are thoughtful.
Also because you cannot die,
we wonder if we can really die,
if our apparent earthly end
means the extinction of our personhood,
of all that we are and have grown to be,
linked with such elegance to so many others
and now, by death, forever separated?
Even the death of other living things
is never extinction but always change.
Awaken us—if you will—
to the hope of an ever-expanding,
even never-ending evolution.
Amen.

If we believe the claims of modern physics, and especially if we harmonize them with O'Murchu's theological subtleties, the story of evolution is a narrative of spiritual adventure and meaning. It is a multidimensional drama full of surprise and promise, sometimes serene, sometimes profoundly chaotic.

For instance, in the evolution of species, records O'Murchu, judging from the fossil record, "There are times of stillness, largely unobserved fertilization and gestation, and then, often suddenly, there is an exuberant outburst of life, frequently assuming an unexpected and totally new structure. Elegance, surprise and creativity dominate the entire process."

"Energy abounds," he says, "Creativity explodes, complexity reorganizes, relationships unfold, and chaos demolishes order—but then strangely tends to beget reorganization. It is difficult to avoid the conclusion that the whole thing is saturated in meaning."

Some writers explain that God has a vision rather than a plan. Living systems on earth require the continual breakdown of any fixed order; this reveals the tragic side of divine innovation. There is always the truth that, in the short term, we cannot be sure all shall be well. Evil, pain, and failure are part of the evolutionary imperative that occasionally moves into forces and forms that are "un-intelligently" designed, shaped by randomness. It is part of human wisdom to acknowledge all these dangers, and plan to cope with them spiritually.

50

All Shall Be Well
—Reaching for Peace of Mind

We know, Spirit Mystery,
that something creative
is happening in our lives all the time,
something good going forward
despite all we worry about.
If even our worst fears came true,
still in your vast resources of artistry
and evolutionary invention
would be some ultimate splendor.
All shall be well in the long run:
that is certainly your decree
and you most probably can make it come about,
for you are God
perhaps not all-mighty but surely all-provident.
Out of the greatest horrors
you can bring perhaps not every good dream,
but every kind of meaningful consummation.
May it be so.

It is important to reflect with gratitude on what it means to be alive and to have a mind. Being alive means to be an organism, one with an essential unity of purpose and action among its parts, a single focus, able to reproduce its kind. By *mind* we mean we are self-reflective, we can meditate, we can invent, we can analyze, we can have knowledge and can know ourselves.

This same aliveness and mental ability seem to some scientists to be qualities of the universe as a whole. The universe seems to them a living organism, with an orderly intelligence. It seems to invent its future, even to heal its wounds. O'Murchu concurs: "Evolution is a story of many strands weaving a complex and elegant tapestry. Information insinuates itself into the universe.... The information ... is itself begotten from within the womb of an alive entity."

At this point the evidence for this theory does not seem compelling, but we do not know enough to eliminate this as a possibility. How otherwise explain the adjustments that our environment makes to cleanse its own oceans, its atmosphere and soil? One thing is certain: without the help and cooperation of the human race, our environment will not be able to save itself from changes that will be catastrophic for all living things.

51

We Rejoice
—In the Joy of Harmony

Mystery surrounding us,
pouring out your benign energies
with prodigality and profligate innovation,
knowing us, nurturing us, caring for us,
receive our prayer of awe and gratitude.
We rejoice to contribute our personal minds
to this elegant universe,
concentrating on creating harmonies this day
with all that exists
amid the music of your benevolent presence everywhere.
We contribute our hearts and our imaginations,
all our bodily energies and all our spiritual resources
to this magnificent evolving reality.
You are with us; we cannot fail.
So be it.

Who are you? Your identification starts with who your parents were, then moves back to grandparents and great-grandparents. Your identity is a series of events, a story that tells you who you are, and you've lived that story from your earliest days. In fact, in a sense you have conversed with the story as you responded to it by acceptance or denial or interpretation.

Now a larger spiritual vision—evolution—locates you within a larger story: the universe story. Science suggests to you that the universe itself claims you as its own and gives you a larger identity.

Do you hear that message? Are you not a child and grandchild of the universe? Is it not part of your very meaning, of your true name, of your identity? O'Murchu challenges us: "Like the mystics of every age, we need to converse also with the creation itself.... It is not just we who tell the story: creation itself is a narrative experience, telling its own story."

52

Conversing with Creation
—When Giving Thanks

Holy Spirit-Force of this creation,
source of life's beginning and end,
we thank you for our story,
honored as we are to be part of your greater story.
We are grateful for our consciousness and our memory,
and for the multiple episodes of our life
in all their ambiguity.
Their ebb and flow make sense in your purview,
and we bless you for your caringness
through all the eons of evolutionary unfolding.
May our story be a worthy part
of a conversation with creation itself,
transparent and meaningful
in a larger context than we can begin to comprehend.
So be it.

The presence of God in us and around us is necessarily constant, but many people claim they can recall particular moments of "visitation," when one's spirits seem enlivened and sparked into excitement by something that felt not so much physical as "other," mystical perhaps, something arriving unprovoked into our consciousness.

The feminist writer Starhawk seems to refer to this in her prayer to the mysterious source of life: "Earth Mother, Star Mother, you who are called by a thousand names, ... you are the embrace that heartens, and the freedom beyond fear." It is that "embrace that heartens" that people describe as mystical for want of a better word.

Some describe it as a sense of "being known" in one's totality, being aware of an all-knowing gaze that is sweetly loving, forgiving, and deeply benign. Aloneness thereafter becomes almost impossible: that mystic presence of God is a permanent part of consciousness. This is not really well described as "holiness" but rather of awareness, of being awake, enlightened. True holiness, on the other hand, has to be marked by heroic choices and stamina, and is almost impossible to discern in a person, having many disguises.

53   *Your Joy, Your Wrath*
—Mystified by Good and Evil

Holy Energy and Love,
we join in your joy
over the pleasure that thrives in the hearts and bodies
of so many living creatures.
Holy Caringness and Wisdom,
we join in your wrath
over the abuse of the vulnerable in this world
and of the vulnerable earth itself.
Holy Spirit of wisdom, energy, and love,
draw us into communion with you
as we live through the mysteries of evil and good
that surround us every day.
Amen.

Our role in evolution is, first of all, to make the universe story our own, as the narrative within which we live. It changes everything for us, makes the world a big, holy place.

We may say that the holiest God we know is the evolutionary God: holiest in the sense of nearest, most awesome, most present. Prior to institutionalized faith, before that formalization of communal spiritual experience that creates a fixed religion, comes personal life experience. That is why writers like O'Murchu recommend, above all, "embracing the story as it unfolds in current paleontological and anthropological research."

In other words, religious people must approach journals like *Scientific American*, *National Geographic*, and *Nature* as spiritual texts. These will make us aware, says O'Murchu, "of the cosmological, evolutionary task we are meant to be about." Our lives of reverence and prayer will make us become citizens of the earth, responsible and responsive as a first obligation to our planet: limiting our use of fossil fuels, saving water, recycling, and promoting food grown without pesticides. It's the lifestyle and spirituality most needed in our world today.

54   *Driving Force*
—Feeling the Call of the Future

Holy Mystery beyond our knowing,
we sense your spirit-power in the evolutionary process
as the driving force
that urges unfolding, complexification, and change
but also as the unimaginable magnetism
calling us to a future
wonderful beyond our dreams.
You are Life, Energy, Beauty, Wisdom,
Impenetrable Mystery.
In humility we praise the wonders of your creation,
and seek only to play our natural
and love-designed role here
in reverence and gratitude.
Amen.

What should each of us be up to in our one human lifetime? In other words, to cite a twentieth-century classic moral ballad: "What's it all about?"

According to O'Murchu, what we need is a wider consciousness: "Our most urgent need today is a new sense of what our universe is about. That more than anything else is what can liberate us from the forces that bind and paralyze us. We must attune ourselves once more to the cosmic womb that begot us."

The Hebrew Scriptures speak eloquently of God's "womb love," that unique feeling a devoted mother has for a child of her womb. (A male writer can only imagine what is meant by this.) What is meant is that rare maternal caringness that is at once physical, spiritual, and perpetual, that continues despite all negative circumstances or barriers to the child's success. We observe it in mothers who, regardless of circumstances, refuse to abandon their children, who encourage and believe in them unconditionally.

That is how, O'Murchu suggests, the cosmos feels about each of us, standing with us in all our dreams and our aspirations for an abundant life that will come from the life force itself. Anything that interferes with our participation in what our universe is really about—and religion may do that—is suspect. Our genuine personal experiences and convictions about what is sacred in life precede in authority any teaching or claim of a religion.

55

Unfolding Miracle
—Honoring Ancestors

We bless you, God of Life,
for the parenting that sparked each of us into existence,
and for the elegant human faculty
that makes possible the storage and transmission
of the genetic code that passes from parent to child,
and for all the yet unnamed forces in creation
that guide our lives and life itself.
We are the children of particular parents
whose genetic information and evolved human traits
we embody,
but we are also the progeny of your own magnificent
unfolding miracle,
programmed to contribute to this evolving miracle
of a cosmos,
and we are grateful to participate
in an exciting, numinous life.
Amen.

Evolution is not a simple, uncomplicated idea. For many it remains a theory, a *perhaps*. To others—most of the scientific community, for instance—it is all but proven, the evidences in the fossil record being conclusive.

How does evolution work—by an outside push, or by constant divine guidance? Or do matter and energy possess an innate evolutionary drive? This latter notion is called co-evolution—which, O'Murchu approvingly reports, "has been adopted by several theorists committed to the view that cosmic evolutionary development is governed primarily by innate self-organizing processes, and not by external mechanistic forces."

Evolution occurs, says Georgetown University theologian John Haught, "because God is more interested in adventure than in preserving the status quo." Here the poetry begins to take off and may soar out of sight for some people. Can we imagine a God who allows randomness and chance as part of creation? For many theologians, that is part of any evolutionary faith.

56

A Larger World
—Seeking Connection

God, Creator of Mystery,
in the growing revelation of reality evolving around us,
we look with gratitude at an ever larger and larger world.
Our personal life has its meaning,
and is dovetailed
in all its co-evolutionary ups and downs
into the larger meaning that encompasses us.
None of us can go it alone: each has innate energies
needed by all.
That whistling cardinal, that burgeoning spruce,
that tearful neighbor, that refugee healed of horror—
all are essential.
We give thanks to be conscious of the awesome narrative
of which we are a part,
paradoxical and baffling as it is and must be,
and commit ourselves to creativity
in cooperating with the forces of life.
Amen.

All of us are mystics, at least potentially, say the theologians. O'Murchu claims as much. What are mystics? Perhaps this label is just a way to identify people we especially admire for their spirituality, or for their instinct for tapping the deeper meaning beneath what is obvious and visible.

A mystical experience is often described as sensing the "one-ness" of everything, the connections between people and the earth, the relationships that hold all living things together in one web of life: or the sense that everything is, in some way, alive—energetic, organized, and valuable.

Each of us has enthusiasms too—for people we love, for cherished animal companions, for powerful events like communal meals and rituals, for experiences of creativity and human connection. To some extent, those enthusiasms embody our spirituality, and if that spirituality encompasses the notion that the world around us is evolving under the influence of mysterious forces, it may be called evolutionary.

At these times of heightened awareness, we inhabit a world of depth, whose surface appearance we can see right through. Beneath what is visible we detect meaning, preciousness, and purpose. At these kinds of moments, we all qualify as mystics. "Faith," says the mystic poet Rabindranath Tagore, "is the bird that feels the light and sings when the dawn is still dark."

"Our God walks with us in the garden of life," says O'Murchu, "the Originating and Sustaining Mystery who is radically transparent to those who have eyes to see."

57

Blessed Be God
—Feeling God's Immediacy

God of Creation,
much of what we observe is radically transparent,
and beneath its thin veil of matter and energy
we can see credible evidence of mind, love, and creativity.
Blessed be your holy name—though we know it not.
Silent Mystery? Ocean of Energy?
Mothering Spirit? Evolutionary God?
We reach ineptly toward you with names.
Still, blessed be your goodness.
Behold, something exists instead of nothing.
Look: a rainbow!
See the starry light from faraway, ancient explosions!
See the bright child, the compassionate neighbor,
the forgiving parent!
Blessed be your love and caringness,
asking only our companionship, our pleasure,
our surrender.
Blessed be God—in all your darkness and mystery.
Amen.

For many people, sadness and failure dominate the earthly scene. It is simply their life experience. Still, the optimistic Teilhard de Chardin found hope on all sides. He wrote, "Blessed be you, mighty matter, irresistible march of evolution, reality ever new-born, you who, by constantly shattering our mental categories, force us to go ever further and further in our pursuit of the truth." He sees meaning even in destroyed hopes, something he frequently grappled with in his own life.

We encounter a great mystery here. Death and shattered hopes seem necessarily a part of every step in the evolution of new life-forms. According to O'Murchu: "New species tend not to evolve without the depletion or deletion of those that previously existed." He cites the scientist/theologians Brian Swimme and Thomas Berry in support of this conviction: the unavoidable role of diminishment and change in the continuing evolution of the cosmos.

We are each a part of something larger than ourselves—how large we can only guess. Our full meaning is in that larger life, and there sometimes is comfort in that larger perspective: our part in a great evolutionary phenomenon.

58

Your Unfolding Forces
—In Times of Disappointment

Holy Creator Spirit,
the memory of disappointments,
of "what might have been,"
brings back sorrow and bewilderment.
We are vulnerable—as you understand so well.
We are easily frayed and wounded,
and often afraid to hope for healing.
In fact, illness threatens us constantly
and saps our energies of creativity and accomplishment.
Yet, around us are your sacraments of hope
great and small:
the night sky full of creative fire, the migrating geese,
the promise-rich crocus of early spring,
the serenity of sleeping infants.
You are here, Holy Mystery, singing in the wind,
comforting us with human laughter,
coloring our life from your rainbow of possibilities
in an evolving world.
Your way is best:
it fills us with hope beyond every sadness.
May it be so.

What we have around us in the cosmos is not just a universe, but a multiverse, if you can believe modern cosmologists. They claim the universe is really more than a million trillion trillion trillion times larger than the already enormous visible cosmos. It's also said to be continually expanding.

"Is this science? Not yet," warns Michael Turner of the University of Chicago. "We can't test it." But we all can ponder it, gaining in awed astonishment what we cannot explain with scientific certitude. According to O'Murchu, there is a thrill in feeling "embraced by the evolving universe itself."

Stephen Hawking said that the farther into space we look, the closer to the beginning we come. Thus it is easy to look backward in time—by using telescopes. And Teilhard de Chardin adds the spiritual note: "Neither in its impetus nor its achievements can science go to its limits without becoming tinged with mysticism."

Our world is spectacular beyond our dreams. Its wonders can be the basis of a contemporary spirituality with room for prayer, doubt, disbelief, and still the highest of hopes.

59

To Be More Creative
—With Thanks for Inspiration

Holy Mind and Energy
behind the magnificent phenomenon of evolution,
we give thanks for our own minds and energies
with their drive toward creativity,
rejoicing in our existence and our functioning.
We would be ever more creative
in expanding our caringness
to include in our care
the whole community of living things,
and even the good of the entire cosmos.
May our hearts embrace each day
the goals of your divine energies,
whatever they are,
and enjoy the thrill of being continuously involved
in something spectacular.
Amen.

We need not wait for death or the fear of it to remind us of God's existence. Ordinary knowledge will do. Einstein said: "The further the spiritual evolution of mankind advances, the more certain it seems to me that the path to genuine religiosity does not lie through the fear of life, and the fear of death, or blind faith, but through striving after rational knowledge."

What lies close around us reveals God's presence. God may be thought of as the aboriginal source of the world's energy, or as the foundational reality beyond all the wonders of love or experience we have known. Metaphorically, we may think of God as a more caring, motherlike mystery than any we encounter in our earthly lives, as a true father more reliable and strong than any father in whose care we may have learned to feel safe and to forge an identity. God may be imagined as our most precious brother, our most loyal sister, our most faithful friend or lover. Still, in the end, the ultimate mystery may remain out of reach—to quote an anonymous medieval mystic—"closer to us than we are to ourselves."

It is helpful to accept at the start that this is not a scientific pursuit but a religious one—in harmony with science. "Science without religion is lame; religion without science is blind," said Einstein. Together, religion and science can strengthen and illuminate the world.

What the Universe Reveals
—When God Is Elusive

Your existence, Holy Intelligence,
our Evolutionary God,
is suggested to us in many basic observable facts:
for instance, that something exists rather than nothing,
or that the elements keep their inner order
despite chaotic forces around them,
or that magnetism affects absolutely everything
including speeding light.
The universe reveals your presence everywhere,
Holy Mystery,
in everything awesome and elegant and true.
Love exists, and attraction, and beauty, and desire,
great invisible forces that permeate our milieu.
You must exist, Source of Everything,
and we rejoice in the ultimate challenge
of that mystery.
Amen.

IV
Prayers of Intimacy

Spirit-power is the ultimate force field that generates and maintains the creativity of the cosmos.

—Diarmuid O'Murchu

I belong to the ranks of devoutly religious men.

—Albert Einstein

An Unfolding Future
—When Feeling Confident

61

Often our prayer to you, Eternal Spirit, begins with the past,
  with memories of people
  whose love has supported us in life,
  sheltering us through every storm of circumstance,
  with gratitude for so many events
  that have warmed our hearts and enriched our days.
Yet ahead there is an unfolding future,
  which is just as remarkable as the past, more so, in fact.
As you have been the empowering spirit of evolution
  for the fifteen billion years of our knowable cosmos,
  so you will energize the future
  with a wealth of events beyond our imaginations.
Our prayers, then, shall turn more often into hope,
  emboldened by what we know of the past.
Guide us on this continuing journey, Holy Creating Love,
  where almost nothing is impossible.
May it be so.

We read in O'Murchu: "My appeal is that we acknowledge [evolution] for what it is, learn to appreciate and understand its mode of operating, allow ourselves to be influenced by its ingenious wisdom, and engage with its dynamic awakening of ever new possibilities for the unfolding future of our universe." If we try this, to "acknowledge evolution for what it is," it may soon feel a little like taking a seat in a railroad car and then noticing that the train is actually moving, almost imperceptively but unmistakably.

Everything we look at in nature—from the flashing red star Sirius and the yawning walls of the Grand Canyon to the instinctual courage of human mothers and the temperature of earth's oceans—though seeming to be fixed and predictable, is unfolding, is in a dynamic state of opening out and changing. That is the evolutionary perspective, and that way of looking at things affects our spirituality and our prayer life. It may multiply our awe, widen our daily world, and even give us hope when hope seems gone.

With Awe and Humility
—In Times of Deep Gratitude

62

Mysterious God,
  with awe and humility
  I observe the colossal dynamics
    of the reality evolving around me:
  the indescribable and sacred events of the past
  and the numinous unfolding of the future
    of which I am forever a part.
I am privileged and blessed to exist,
  blessed to possess knowledge of where I came from,
  blessed to have solid hopes
  for a future of meaning
  and the community of those I love.
See in my heart my gratitude
  for all your mysterious gifts of energy and blessing.
Amen.

People find it instinctive to place their hand on their heart at thoughtful moments: to sing the national anthem, to pledge allegiance to the flag—or when they suddenly feel grateful. It works easily as a prayer also: when we wish to express thanks to the Great Mystery in which we live but find words inadequate or impossible. God "sees us always," we might say, or "knows us" in an all-seeing, loving gaze.

So the gesture of hand-on-heart constitutes a prayer that's easy to communicate to God and instantly received. If your mind is hummingbird-like, rather than still, the simple gesture is particularly comforting, since it remains in place while the imagination may fly off in a dozen other directions. You feel that your prayer persists.

Battery-powered human action figures—those popular children's toys—sometimes have a button on the figure's chest that lights them up in the dark: a helpful paradigm for this simple prayer. You place your hand on your heart and simply light up. You give thanks to God with a gesture. Pedestrian as this piety is, it can be full of comfort and usefulness when all else fails.

You Know My Name
—Feeling Intimate Hope

63

Holy Spirit within and near me:
  you know every experience of each of my senses.
Your divine memory comprehends
  and encompasses my own memory,
  your all-knowing eyes read my DNA—
  three billion digits long—
  like a single unpronounceable word,
  with all my promise and meaning laid out there.
That is my truest name, who I am, and you alone know it.
It is a joy to be so known,
  for your gaze is also loving and caring:
  I am your creation, your very child.
See then my unfolding life today, my unfolding beauty,
  my evolving self,
  my whole "becoming"
  empowered by your original creative act,
  the initiation that brought my complex selfhood into being,
  its projections guiding my development through time
  into the unique and elegant event, trajectory, and story
  that is my existence and identity.
Therefore I give thanks, however feebly—
  but less and less feebly
  as, with your own explosive energies,
  I expand into the galaxy of my full identity
  and soar toward the horizon of full selfhood.
May it be so.

Writers on evolution and the environment often state that humankind should not be considered a species of life superior to other animals but rather as just one of the equal parts of the web of life and of the earth's ecosystem. A misconceived "human superiority" has proved to be dangerous: humans easily become deluded and think of themselves as owners— not stewards and caretakers—of the earth, ruling over animals who presumably have no rights at all, and free to use earthly resources with no sense of responsibility to all life's needs in the future.

The full truth may well lie somewhere in the middle, between superior and equal. While the human capacity for language and creativity seem like gifts notably superior to those of other animals, humans must relate to the rest of creation with reverence, feeling their intimate connection and mutual relatedness to everything else. Dogs companion the blind. Horses assist loggers. Cats warm the heart. All the musical parts of the earth symphony are in one sense equal, and essential. Yet, in creation, perhaps it is the animals capable of self-reflection, wonder, and language that carry a heavier responsibility to sustain the life web for the benefit of all.

You Are Real

—When Knowing God's Closeness

64

You are real, Most Holy Mystery:
  though invisible, silent, and even at times out of reach.
You are real, the source of all that is.
In one perspective you are the end-product of reasoning,
  an arm's length as it were
  from my powers of touch and scent,
  of sight and hearing,
  yet as real as anything available to my senses.
Nothing else in life would make sense without you,
  Holy Presence,
  and with you, everything can make sense.
Still more comforting than such reasoning
  is the consensus of humankind,
  and even closer than that
  is my heart's consciousness of your presence,
  your gaze, your mind, your mystery,
  your evolutionary urgings.
Holy God, be ever more real to me
  that I may be ever more your useful servant
  and co-creator of this evolving world.
Amen.

The special contribution of mystics like Teilhard de Chardin is to help shape a new human attitude toward reality. In O'Murchu's words: "It is in their ability to see with breadth and depth that mystics contribute to the transformation of consciousness. They keep us focused on the larger picture and challenge us to engage with the deeper question."

Teilhard was best characterized as a "panentheist," and he was not the only one. Many people today feel exactly the same way, not that everything is divine (pantheism) but that the divine is in everything (panentheism). It is commonplace to name God "Mystery surrounding us" because that may be how it feels. People experience being surrounded by divinity, submerged in God the way fish are submerged in water—but with a difference: the water does not penetrate every part of the fish as God does us.

Such categorical names are not always helpful and are seldom precise. But if you feel panentheisic, like resting in a God who exists in every part of you, do so. Soak, if you wish—to the bone, to the center—in the deeply satisfying presence of the Universal Mystery. It's another word for prayer.

Serious about Death
—In Discomfort of Mind

65

I want to be serious about death, Holy Creator,
   because it is you I turn to when I turn to that thought.
Still, something in the human psyche
   promotes a denial of uncomfortable facts,
   and death is certainly one of those.
Protect me, if you can, from delusionary thinking.
At death I expect to be—as I have been all along—
   safe in your evolutionary mystery,
   one I do not expect to comprehend completely
   even at death.
Meanwhile, give me eyes wide open to all that is
   and all that is illusory,
   patience with my necessary questioning,
   and an instinct for what is true.
Amen.

A commonplace Buddhist principle is that impermanence is an essential part of everything. But when you say that "nothing *is* permanent," you state something you do not know for sure. It is not provable. It's unscientific, an educated guess, a theory. Similarly, to claim that "the human spirit lives on after death" is to state as true something you do not know scientifically. To be accurate, you must say "the human spirit *seems* immortal." It is important even for scientists to distinguish what can be tested and proven true from what may possibly be true as an explanation of mysterious physical phenomena.

The immortality of the soul seems possible and even likely to most people on earth and throughout history—partly out of wishful thinking but also partly out of our experience of the energies of human beings. After all, scientifically, nothing is ever totally destroyed, only changed into something else. All scientists accept that. We have no scientific evidence for the total extinction of any matter or energy.

Aboriginal peoples—who presumably learn their spiritual attitudes from nature—instinctively assume that all the people they know and love go into some other level of existence when they die. This not only makes "natural" and even scientific sense: it helps solve the anomaly of the obvious unfairness of life. How else—they might ask—are we to trust the world and see it as ultimately benign? Only if a balancing fairness comes along in another existence. It's possible; some would say likely. No one *knows.*

An Idea You Love
—Facing the Mysteries of Life and Death

66

The unknown lies all around me, Holy Creator Mystery, my
　　God:
　　and nothing more is unknown than yourself:
　　your name, your dreams, your evolutionary purposes.
It is in puzzling over the meaning of my existence
　　that I often find my way to you.
　　Why do I exist?
　　It may seem that I exist
　　because I am an idea, a story, you love.
　　　　That is plausible, but is there more?
　　In my creativity, am I a co-inventor of the future,
　　　　sharing with You in shaping the world,
　　in wondering appreciatively at the cosmos?
　　Is my existence temporary—as it appears—
　　　　or immortal—as I sometimes hope?
I have a longing to understand these mysteries.
This longing empowers me to search,
　　and through that energy of longing
　　I often discover a sense of your guiding presence.
I give thanks for the unremitting will-to-meaning I have:
　　it empowers my heart and makes my faith in you,
　　Holy Parenting Spirit, possible—
　　and inevitable.
Amen.

Rabbi Joshua Liebman in the mid-twentieth century wrote the bestseller *Peace of Mind,* in which he tellingly makes the case for some kind of "immortality" after death. He gathers testimonies in favor of this theory from Plato, Kant, Tolstoy, Montaigne, and others. "Even such a realistic philosopher as William James," says Liebman, "who had long been disinterested in the question of immortality, in the last few years of his life began to believe in its possibility. When asked why, he said, 'Because I am just becoming fit to live.'"

Wrote Teilhard in *Activation of Energy:* "What is most vitally necessary to the thinking earth is faith, and a great faith, and ever more faith. To know that we are not prisoners; to know that there is a way out: that there is air, and light, and love somewhere beyond the reach of all death; to know this, to know that it is neither an illusion nor a fairy tale; that—if we are not to perish smothered in the very stuff of our being—is what we must at all costs secure. And it is there that we find what I may well be so bold as to call the evolutionary role of religions."

More Than My Creator
—In an Expansive Mood

67

Holy God of my life, knowing me and my history
   in its every detail,
   because you care about everything I do,
   you are more than my creator
   and sustaining sacred presence,
   and my future:
you center me,
   since you are the center of, or the relational matrix of,
   all of cosmic reality.
You, Creating Spirit,
   hold in your divine caringness
   all space and time, all stars and galaxies of stars,
   all light and fire, all life and intelligence.
My God and my All,
   you are also the God of all that is, has been, and can be.
Out of my diminutive but crucial life and heart
   I give you gratitude.
May all your creative dreams come true, Incomprehensible
   Mystery,
   my God, and God of All.
Amen.

New approximations published by London's Royal Astronomical Society in 2003 set the number of stars at seventy million million million times the number that are visible. That is seven followed by twenty-two zeros. One astronomer estimated that is more than there are grains of sand on every beach and desert on earth.

It is indeed a large world and universe we live in, much larger than we can imagine. Still it is undoubtedly all one reality. Thomas Berry makes the point that "there is eventually only one story; ... nothing is itself without everything else." We may feel lost in the stars, but we may find ourselves there too: star-children, living amid star-dust, created in star-fire, and—if we are wise enough to have hope as large as our prospects—starry-eyed.

Science writer Brian Swimme notes that our present generation is the first one to know that "our ancestry stretches back through the life-forms and into the stars, back to the beginning of the primeval fireball," to realize that "this universe is a single, multiform, energetic unfolding of matter, mind, intelligence and life." This consciousness may be the most hopeful "catholicism" or internationalism of the future, the ultimate one-world-building revelation brought down not from Mount Sinai but from the lofty discoveries of scientists. This may be a very helpful spirituality that can make sense for a world community pulled violently apart by religious differ-ences, and threatened with worldwide ecological disaster and extinction.

Spirit of Life
—Feeling Deep Thankfulness

68

Spirit of Life, enlivening vital force within me,
  if there is any inspiration or enthusiasm in me this day,
  it is your evolutionary energies at work,
  thrusting me each moment into being,
  targeting my heart and selfhood toward a positive destiny,
  working within my vital organs and soul center
    to empower me to selfhood
    at every one of my life's moments,
  drawing me constantly into communion with others
  and on into the unlimited future of the universe.
I give thanks for who I am and have become,
  with trusting surrender to my destiny.
Amen.

The act of "selving" is poet Gerard Manley Hopkins's idea of—and invented word for—the crucial human act. At age twenty-two he sketched from a low bridge his own face reflected in a lake, surely wondering about what kind of man he saw down there, never dreaming he might be sketching a poet to be immortalized in a plaque on the floor of Westminster Abbey next to Shakespeare, Milton, and Wordsworth.

Eighteen years later, he put the same puzzlement into humming and soaring words in the final eight lines of a sonnet. Hopkins writes—in his signature polyphony of rhythm and rhyme:

> As kingfishers catch fire, [as] dragonflies draw flame,
> as tumbled over rim in roundy wells
> stones ring; like each tucked string tells, each hung bell's
> bow swung finds tongue to fling out broad its name;
> each mortal thing does one thing and the same:
> deals out that being indoors each one dwells,
> selves—goes itself; *myself* it speaks and spells,
> crying *What I do is me: for that I came.*

O'Murchu describes the evolving self as empowered both by the force of the prodigious Big Bang and by our autonomous inner powers. He speaks eloquently of the role of evolution in developing our most authentic self, and of the need to "appropriate our evolutionary story and reconnect … with the enlivening Spirit."

Keep Us Awake
—Knowing a Limitless Presence

In your presence, infinite Mystery,
    I feel the influence of a deep vision,
    one treasured and shared by the mystics of every age and
    religion,
    by instinct-gifted children, and the insightful poor.
"Everything is a part of everything else": amazing!
You, Holy God, are present not only everywhere,
    but also in the forgotten past
    and throughout the unlimited future.
Holy Mystery, our God.
    keep us illumined by that perspective.
Spirit of the evolving world,
    persuade us to courage
    in pursuing what is true and desirable,
    whatever its cost.
Amen.

PART IV

The keynote of all mysticism is oneness, unity, to suddenly discover "Aha!": diversity is ultimately "sameness after all." We all look for oneness in the midst of multiplicity, with philosophical minds even hoping to someday find the "core" of everything.

That core may be called love, or elegance, or energy, or life, or even wisdom. The mystic finds it, and surrenders to it. It is crucial, for instance, for children to recognize and appreciate diversity early, to know people from diverse cultures and races, as well as gay and lesbian people, and transgender men and women, who are walking sacraments of diversity, invention, and surprise.

It is a blessing for children to have this wide, wide world of diversity ahead of them so they can find their own place, however innovative or unexpected that may be, where they can accept themselves for whoever they are, where they can learn to trust their experience rather than embracing someone's theory or their culture's prejudgments.

Hopefully, they will find through their own brand of mysticism "sameness after all." Whatever kind of human invention they encounter or discover themselves to be, they do fit in, they must fit in, for they are part of this one reality. Children have far less trouble than adults seeing an ultimate sameness, so they are ready to experience diversity early. It's the best education you can give them.

In Pain
—When Life Skills Fail

70

I am in pain before you, holy Wisdom-Force, God of my
  heart.
My efforts to harmonize with those I love
  are not satisfactory or effectual.
Grace me with greater insight, teach me to care more wisely.
Yours are the essential energies
  that promote the evolution of life-giving relationships.
I depend at this moment on those energies and on your spirit.
May your gracious presence be with me
  as I put my trust in your unfolding creation.
Around me are so many creative wonders
  and marvels of invention.
May my own heart's serenity—
  or at least my peaceful resignation—
  be another of your creations.
You are God: can you make it happen?
It is my prayer.
May it be so.

The prophetic Shakti Gawain in *Creating True Prosperity* wrote: "Life is always attempting to move us in the direction of our own evolution and development.... Every experience and event of our lives is part of that process."

From O'Murchu we can add: "The divine is first and foremost a wisdom-force, forging unceasingly the relationships that sustain and enhance life."

Remarks like these lead us to surmise that the Big Bang was a bigger bang than is normally assumed. What exploded outward in what Thomas Berry described as that "primordial flaring-forth" was not only the solid objects that populate the cosmos today and the energies within and pro-pelling them, but also the surging forces of expanding and evolving life that operate in every earthen plant and animal, drawing forward its complexifi-cation and adaptation, and the drive underlying every living desire and appetite for knowledge within plants and animals, including human animals.

O'Murchu adds the conviction that the Big Bang "is not ... a one-time event but ... an unceasing process." When you observe an infant reaching out to experience the feel of a rubber ball or a kitten, it is an extension of that sacred explosion at the beginning of time and space.

Prayer of Anguish
—Facing an Ominous Threat

71

Holy Mystery beneath the astonishing evolution
   sparkling around us,
    hear my prayer of anguish and contrition
    for the human misuse of your colossal gifts
    that are necessary for life on earth.
Misuse is a mild word for it:
   our defiling of air, soil, and water
    is also reckless imprudence
    and calamitous shortsightedness.
Inspire us all—if you can—
   to swiftly repair the damage we have done
    to our earthen home and environment
    so we may hand to our children a hope-filled future,
    and not a catastrophe.
Amen.

A layer of ozone screens us from deadly ultraviolet rays coming to the earth from the sun. This protective screen is being eroded, scientists say, by emissions in the air from fuels overused by humans—especially in power plants and motor vehicles. This leads inevitably to increased skin cancers and other illnesses.

In the fall of 2003 U.S. federal researchers reported that the size of the ozone hole over Antarctica that year was the second-largest ever recorded. It covered 10½ million square miles, an area larger than North America.

We have to face the fact now that all life on earth is under catastrophic threat—but unbelievably our government finds it inconvenient to pay attention to it. The world of our children and of their children is being jeopardized.

Other evidence of this abounds: because of global warming, the permafrost in arctic Canada is melting—something that it was thought would never happen. Millions of tons of poisonous arsenic dust are stored in that permafrost beneath the gold mines near the Great Slave Lake, Canada's largest lake, and a local environmental catastrophe is imminent. Already, fishing in the lake is compromised by poisons from the melt.

This is no doubt the most pressing political cause there is, affecting the entire earth and the whole human race. Unless it is addressed and remedied, the catastrophe will smother all the evolutionary advances that have produced life and return the earth to its primitive lifeless state.

No Real Name
—Privileged to Exist

72

I have no real name for you, Holy Mystery,
Spirit-Force at work in my life and all around me,
Holy Energy at the heart of evolution,
    active in every cell and atom within me,
    and co-creating with me the world I live in,
    from the center of my consciousness
    out to the very ends of the unfinished cosmos.
But do you have a name for me?
    There is no need for one:
    you know me perfectly
    in every detail of my DNA, through all my past,
    and especially in all my potential for the future.
It is a privilege to express simple gratitude
    for this relationship with you,
    for this large existence,
    to feel myself unfolding within your mystery,
    and a joy to be part of it.
Amen

Given names are identifiers tagged on to us arbitrarily. The name other people know us by could be totally different. On the other hand, the full sequence of the human genome is a string of three billion letters, composed of a four-letter alphabet, and containing the complete recipe for building and running a human body. This gigantic "word" is our real name, our only nonarbitrary identity. It is also a name God alone knows and can, in a sense, utter.

Medieval philosophers believed that each created thing's existence would not continue without God's continuous creating word. In their understanding, one would not be sustained in existence without God's continuous utterance of the unpronounceable name that is you, a name echoed in almost unthinkable detail in every cell of your human body.

Your Larger Story
—Confident in the Future

73

Your larger story, holy God,
   gives me a new cosmic perspective.
What happens to me in life is not a final consideration.
My personal "judgment day" is not ultimate:
I am a part of a greater drama,
   and I have a meaningful, if small, role to play in it.
May your evolutionary dream for this earth come true
   as it surely will, irresistible Creator.
May your loving reign prevail, as many prophets have prayed
   and taught others to pray.
I hand over my own story
   to the Universe Story unfolding around me,
   and rejoice to find my meaning there,
   believing that, in the greater picture, all shall be well,
   even magnificent, in the end.
Amen.

Albert Einstein once wrote: "A human being is a part of a whole, something called by us a universe, a part limited in time and space. He experiences himself, his thoughts and feelings, as something separated from the rest, [which is] a kind of optical delusion of his consciousness. This delusion is a kind of prison for us, restricting us to our personal desires and to affection for a few persons nearest to us. Our task must be to free ourselves from this prison by widening our circle of compassion to embrace all living creatures and the whole of nature in its beauty."

A famous Buddhist meditation accomplishes this, summoning up first compassion for someone very dear to us, then spreading that feeling to a wider circle of acquaintances, and finally widening the circle of compassion to include the whole earth community.

All this spirituality may be delusional if we live essentially in isolation from the human race, as do many of the safely cloistered clergy and the overly privileged in select communities. Evolution moves us instead toward community and communion, and we cooperate best with its energies when we honor the less privileged by living where they live, knowing their stories, taking their side in political struggles, and respecting and responding to their needs. This is nothing more than the golden rule: doing unto others as we would have them do unto us, a moral principle known in every single religion on earth.

Servant of Your Presence 74
—Longing to Know God

Holy Creator, Spirit-Force in this evolving universe,
    if you exist—and you do—
    then you must want to be known—
    and not theoretically but personally—
as the goal of each personal trajectory,
as the spiritual inspiration within all the world's compassion,
as the inventor of the lovingness
    of every caring mother or father,
    friend, sibling, or lover,
    wanting to be known in your effects,
    known in your elusive goodness and hidden love,
    a presence beneath and within culture and spirituality:
    a God of wisdom and love and inventiveness.
Let me become—in however small a way—
    a servant of your energies to those around me
    as others have played that role in my own life.
Make me an instrument of your presence as well as of your
    peace.
Amen.

The language of modern physics clashes with the conventional mind. Author Philip Simmons in his contemporary classic *Learning to Fall* gives this confusing summary of one baffling phenomenon in physics: "Things wink in and out of being as light becomes matter and matter light." Ordinary academic metaphysics, the study of "being," cannot deal at all with such a concept. An awed Annie Dillard likes the summary phrase of her physicist friend speaking of the subatomic world: "Everything that has already happened is particles; everything in the future is waves."

Indetermination seems to be the key here. Somehow or other the reality around us—if we look deeply—is essentially changeable, able to confound our imaginings. The Buddhists call it an essential impermanence that beautifully harmonizes with modern physics, where in quantum mechanics infinitesimal particles move in and out of existence. In the view of Teilhard de Chardin, the universe is simply radically unfinished, and thus must be constantly changing.

God of Immense Goodness,
    prayers for favors arise from our hearts
    even when our heads tell us it's futile.
Our reasoning is correct—
    an all-compassionate God
    cannot become more compassionate—
    but our instinct overrides it:
    you are God, why won't you help?
You are all-good, why aren't you all-mighty?
Surely wishful thinking is not totally bad—
    provided we can laugh at ourselves,
    and reverence your sovereignty,
    while keeping faith
    in the incalculable outpouring of love that this creation is
    prior to any prayers of ours to improve it.
May it be so.

Life changed after 9/11 for Americans—because suddenly we all felt unthinkably vulnerable and newly threatened. But bad as it was, the World Trade Center catastrophe did not threaten tidal waves a mile high "racing around the globe again and again" followed by a wipeout of all life on earth, all of which once happened. Recently the magazine *Science* ran a story about the discovery of the evidence of just such a global disaster. Long ago an asteroid, twelve miles wide, actually hit the earth not far from the United States, and virtually all life on earth ceased to exist, most notably that of the dinosaurs who had thrived on almost every continent.

Could it happen again? It could. Scientists estimate that some thirty thousand large asteroids threaten the earth all the time. In *Scientific American* it was recently reported that "on an average night more than 100 million pieces of interplanetary debris enter Earth's atmosphere. Luckily, most of these bits of asteroids and comets are no bigger than small pebbles." This amounts to a rain—of rocks—which earthlings can never come in out of. The larger ones end up as shooting stars, of course, burned up in the earth's atmosphere.

That rain of rocks also prompts a rain of questions. Is this reality really benevolent toward life? Is it out of control? Could we not all be dead tomorrow? today? Should we not be more ready for such a finale?

Had we realized the possibility of 9/11, would we not have changed our level of preparedness? Once we realize our constant danger from asteroids, should we not live differently? Were we truly wise, we would live as if death could come at any moment—which might give us a greater impulse for contact with our evolutionary God, the only one there is.

Wonderful Universe
—Feeling the Ecstasy of Existence

Holy Spirit, our Creator and Sustainer,
   receive my thanks for finding myself alive
   here in a universe wonderful beyond my wildest dreams,
     and possibly even itself alive and intelligent;
   and for my role in its colossal story
   that, while engaging me intimately
   in events of cosmic import,
   gives me a new and more holistic access
   to truth and wonder.
Teach me to integrate the co-creativity
   of an evolutionary faith
   even into a pedestrian life.
Amen.

According to some experts in the field of science and spirituality, the universe itself seems somehow alive and intelligent, caring about everything that happens with a great cosmic affection, healing injuries to itself, planning a spectacular future. Others see this contention as extravagant, a fanciful possibility but without sufficient empirical evidence to establish its validity.

O'Murchu speaks sympathetically of this theory, of the notion of "an alive universe that is innately intelligent." It's an idea worth contemplating. "Nothing is too wonderful to exist," said Michael Faraday, the discoverer of electromagnetism. On these grounds, almost everything we can dream up—that is not itself a contradiction—is possible.

"The purpose of every story," says O'Murchu, "is to break open our conventional views of reality, to orient us to a larger reality with a more holistic aperture for truth." The Universe Story achieves that aim stunningly.

Wise Creating Spirit around me and within me,
   I bless you for the elegant unfolding beauty of creation
   taking place at this moment,
   and for what that evolution reveals to me about you:
      your steady energies and caringness,
      the dance of your ambiguous self-revelation,
      your choice to remain largely unknown.
I give you thanks for things as they are,
   and harmonize as best I can with you
   and the evolving forces of life,
   welcoming my role as appreciative audience.
Amen.

It is difficult to discern what is going on in the world. "The cosmos reveals itself," says John Haught, "as an adventure of continual experimentation with novel forms of order. Hence, being part of this cosmos already means being a participant in a momentous adventure story."

O'Murchu summarizes this phenomenon as an "evolutionary unfolding governed by the allurement of the future."

However we think of it, evolution is a mind-blowing thought that can put us in a new world.

Part of our life role is to be celebrants and appreciators of the astonishing beauty and drama of the cosmic story unfolding around us and in us. Unless we do that, we fail in our part of it all. The drama going on before our eyes on earth is not some kind of theater of the absurd or dress rehearsal where no audience is needed. Rather, what is happening is an irreversible and unrepeatable epic drama that tells us of the colossal outpouring goodness of the sacred life force, of the goodness of this indescribably elegant mystery that is the creative Spirit and Energy we sometimes call God. That's what's going on.

But how to explain, then, the meaningfulness of most of creation's lengthy and elegant cosmological drama? Where was the audience? Logic suggests there was one but tells us no more. The late Carl Sagan in his film *Contact* put the following testimonial into the mouth of a key character: "I had an experience ..., a vision of the universe ... that tells us we belong to something that is greater than ourselves, that we are not—that none of us—are alone." How little of what's going on do we know!

God in Hiding

—Cherishing God's Energies

78

Spirit of God, in almost perfect hiding,
I welcome you to enter my work from your darkness.
Out of the rushing river of your energies
   active in everything that is
   comes the irresistible glowing warmth
   of your magnetic purposes in me.
You discern perfectly what I am about,
   you lure me with a future
   of endless evolutionary possibility.
Let me harmonize my singular melody
   with the colossal chorus of all creation,
   in all space, and in all time,
   so that what I do promotes the evolution of your desires
   and what you desire
   grows as a discernible pattern beneath my efforts.
Amen.

Ritual has a powerful hold on the human mind, and the international celebrations of Earth Day have already had a powerful effect on consciousness, convincing people subconsciously—but worldwide—of the preciousness of our one vulnerable planet.

Is it time to inaugurate a celebration of the Big Bang? This is an idea of O'Murchu's, who describes it as "a wonderful explosion and proliferation of possibility, deserving remembrance." We are not only one earth but one universe. The Earth Story is indeed our planetary story, but our truest story began long before the Earth Story, in the primal explosion that science dubs the Big Bang. Some scientists even claim to hear echoes of that explosion today in the uniform background hiss detectable throughout space.

One possibility for a celebration date in the northern hemisphere would be the day of the summer solstice, that most lightsome day reminding us of the very birth of light, the Big Bang. A worldwide consciousness of the Big Bang would deepen our planetary drive toward global unity and increase our consciousness of our permanent debt of gratitude to God or to the Universe or just to reality.

Evolving Future
—Grateful for Awakening

79

Despite my painful hours and days,
    I discern a mystery of love in your world, Creating Spirit.
Blessed am I.
We have evolved into people tied together by bonds of love,
    human magnetism linking us
    and empowering us above and beyond ourselves.
We all admire individuals, we deeply cherish some of them,
    we are forever tied to others: children, parents, lovers.
All these forces are invisible as air but as undeniable also.
    Is not all this the inner wisdom of reality
    awakening us to our elegance and our possibilities?
I give thanks for love, Holy God,
    and renew my faith in the evolving future.
So be it.

Wisdom is a highly charged word with many meanings. Usually it applies to a person who has extensive knowledge and a strong commitment to it. When a philosopher uses *wisdom* poetically to describe the elegance of something in its purposes and form, wisdom conveys an illuminating view.

The forces of love in the world, for instance, can be called wisdom: an awesome phenomenon that achieves great good and is hard to describe in nonmetaphorical terms. *Evolutionary Faith* states it this way: "The power of wisdom seems to emerge from within. It erupts from the depths, sometimes gently and unobtrusively ..., at other times with a wild, passionate exuberance.... Wisdom animates and awakens rather than governs as if by external force." Einstein said: "More and more I come to value charity and love of one's fellow being above everything else; all our lauded technological progress, our very civilization, is like the axe in the hand of the pathological criminal." Theologian Elizabeth Johnson, in a recent book review for *America* magazine, calls the evolution of the cosmos "an extravagantly sacramental expression of a transcendent, personal, divine power always opening up a future for the world."

No description of the universe and of its "wisdom" can be adequate. We live in the midst of something beautiful and elegant beyond description.

To Have a Part
—Honored to Participate

80

I give thanks, Holy Mystery,
    to have a part in this evolutionary phenomenon,
    and to strive for communion with all life,
    however diverse and bewildering,
    to be alive and conscious
    in the midst of an unfolding universe
    whose existence stretches back
    an almost unthinkable passage of time,
    across an almost inconceivable ocean of space.
To know my own true name this day
    is to recognize myself to be your creature, your child,
    your very hope and promise,
    and to pledge myself as faithfully as I can
    to celebrate my part in this colossal drama
    with passion and humility.
Amen.

TO HAVE A PART

Remembering Loveliness
by Mary Goergen, OSF

… We should celebrate.
We are about to enter the 15 millionth millennium of the universe.
We are about to enter the 4.5 millionth millennium of the earth.
We are about to enter the 4 millionth millennium of life.
We are about to enter the 2,600th millennium of humans.
We are entering the 4th millennium of recorded history.

We are who we are today—because of all that has existed before us.
We carry in our bodies and spirits the struggles and changes, joys
and sorrows, loves and hates that have occurred throughout all time.

We are called to live with the knowledge and awareness that we are
part of all that is, and that our decisions have an effect on the quality
of life for all beings. We are called to live this connectedness that
exists between all members of creation. We are called to put our
hands on creation and speak to it in words and touch, telling it how
lovely it is—because it cannot remember. We are called to remember
loveliness for one another until each of us can remember, believe, and
live in that love.

Afterword

In this very useful volume, William Cleary offers a prayerful overview of the major themes explored in my book *Evolutionary Faith*. Themes of gratitude and appreciation of God's goodness feature strongly. The nature of these prayers, however, also invites some fresh reflections on the meaning of prayer itself and our desire for more relevant prayer experiences in our daily lives. Who finds prayer easy? Very few. We need all the help we can get.

Story as Prayer

The study of evolution—cosmic, planetary, human—has been heavily influenced by Darwinian theory, with the conventional understanding of life forces battling to survive and outlive the weaker variants. But several contemporary scholars transcend this narrow, mechanistic view. Beyond the facts that can be quantified and verified is a story that is both complex and elegant. The story is peppered with "unknowns" and contains paradoxes and contradictions. But it is susceptible to an investigation that opens us up to mystery and wonder, sentiments that can be called prayer. Mystics have known this transparency of nature since time immemorial.

It is this mystical element in prayer that awakens silence, awe, and trust. Despite all the paradoxes and contradictions, something deep inside convinces us that our relationship with the profound mystery is fundamentally benign. The narrowly rational mind of this age—and every age—cannot grasp or comprehend this message and is excessively preoccupied with control, and this is the very thing that nature does not yield to.

Despite all the advances of science and technology, the creation that surrounds us is largely out of our control, and beyond our human capacity to be in charge. Something bigger, deeper, and more mysterious is at stake. Only the prayerful heart can discern the deeper meaning and the unfolding story that has endured over billions of years.

We may assume that for millennia, back into our prelinguistic existence, humans have told stories. Storytelling is one of the oldest means we have known through which we grappled with the encompassing mystery. And the prophetic figures of all the great religions resort to the power of story. The words and story events are merely the vehicle. The enlightenment of mind and spirit happens through the engagement with imagination, intuition, and articulation using word, symbol, gesture, and ritual. Story-communication is fundamentally a prayer-form, defying and transcending all our efforts at mere rational analysis.

No matter how secular or trivial the context, storytelling always embodies a search for meaning and integration. We tell stories to transcend the threat of meaninglessness. As a species we have yet to come to terms with the original inspiration for story-telling itself. Strictly speaking, it is not a human invention; it may be thought of as an endowment of the creative universe, unraveling its own story in stars and galaxies, planets and quasars, mountains and rivers, bacteria and fireflies, primates and humans, over billions of years. In a way, creation itself is the primordial story that begets every story ever told. It is not humans who invented stories, then; creation did so, many eons ago.

All the great religions, in various forms, allude to this primordial story, attributing its power to the divine energy that animates and sustains everything. We have until now seldom taken this religious insight seriously. And ironically, we may even have to admit that today it is the secular sciences, rather than the religious creeds and dogmas, that are reawakening us to the mysterious universe within which we live and move and have our being—and our role.

The Role of Silence

Ordinary prayers tend to be spoken or written in words, as are those in the present volume. The words are useful, but silence is even more essential. When prayers allude to, or describe, the divine at work in creation, spaces and interludes between the words need to be created for creation to speak for itself. The words provide a medium through which we access the deeper mystery and become acquainted with its nourishing graciousness. But the words are merely the touchstone that stirs the heart and alerts the mind to something a great deal more profound.

When the words give way to the story, when we find ourselves awakened and participating in the midst of a great narrative, then prayer truly happens. Then, it is not so much we who pray; rather, the creative vitality of God awakens contemplative prayerfulness in our hearts. We begin to see things differently, and may even be disturbingly challenged to forgo those external props—the words—which previously seemed essential. We're beginning to see as God sees, and to understand with the eyes of the heart. In the great religions, this experience is known as contemplation.

Underestimating the Mystery

Of all the revolutionary discoveries explored in the new physics, none is more awesome than our fresh understanding of energy-flow. Everything in creation is born out of energy. Science tends to describe the process whereby energy is used or measured but refuses to speculate on its nature. Theology tends to attribute its origin to a divine creator—outside and beyond creation, often underestimating the mystery within which our daily lives are immersed.

Ever since the time of the ancient Greeks (and I suspect long before it), humans have questioned the nature of empty space. We have long intuited that it carried secrets of enormous significance for our daily existence. Quantum physics highlights the incredible potential of this apparently vacuous nothingness. Yet, out of the emptiness of creation come every form and structure we see around us. The emptiness is a fertile resource, seething with creativity. And there is also growing evidence to suggest that creation needs these enormous stretches of "empty space"—over 90 percent of the known cosmos—for everything to function in creative interdependence.

Praying within this emptiness has been a recurring theme in mystical literature. The emphasis tends to be on the God whose significance we glean through absence rather than presence. This is the spiritual experience often alluded to as the dark night of the soul. What modern science is highlighting, however, is not absence but presence. There is an intensity in the creative vacuum, strongly indicative of prodigious fertility and inexhaustible resourcefulness.

What does the practice of prayer mean in this context? Primarily we are experiencing sentiments of awe and wonder arising from the inner depths of the soul. It is the precondition for the prayer of praise, sometimes articulated in words, but often transcending the power of words. Silence rather than word is the response most frequently evoked, a silence that is more likely to translate into stillness and solitude, or, alternatively, into creative movement, for instance, a dance, a communal gesture, or an artistic expression rather than word formulas. This, in fact, may be the oldest form of prayer known to our species, one that predates formal religion by many thousands of years.

Relationality

What distinguishes quantum theory from the classic formulations of science is the emphasis on relationship, sometimes described as interdependence or interconnectedness. In the older, classic worldview, everything has to be independent, autonomous, explainable in its own right, distinct from everything else. Hence the preoccupation with such things as the basic building blocks of matter.

However, from the quantum perspective, nothing makes sense in isolation. Nature is perceived as a network of interconnections, governed by the principle that the whole is greater than the sum of the parts. It holds. At the operational level, it is the interconnections that enable things to happen, while the existence of each individual organism is governed by a relational power at a higher level.

Once again, we encounter an ancient belief long known to, and cherished by, our ancestors. We see it articulated in the concept of a divine three-ness, which, in various expressions, occurs in all the major world religions. The meaning of reality on the grand scale is understood to arise from its connections, from a relational matrix, which experientially our ancestors knew for thousands of years. In time, that primordial experience was translated into the various threefold understandings of the divine in the various religions.

Prayer, therefore, may be thought of as the awareness of, and response to, this relational dynamic. Prayer is itself a mode of interconnection, a desire to relate at a deeper level. Prayer is not so much an activity on a particular day as a disposition that exposes the soul to relational energy and cultivates the capacity to relate to everything more lovingly and more meaningfully. Prayer is a kind of glue that helps us to keep reality as a magnificent whole, despite all the paradoxes and contradictions that characterize creation.

Our capacity to relate is always spiritual. This does not necessarily mean that it is always destined for a good outcome. Light and darkness intermingle in the archetypal realm, that deep place within us and within the whole of creation where everything is interconnected. By the same token, relationships are not just about or between people. Humans are endowed with a capacity to relate because the whole of creation is essentially relational. Humans can only become truly relational beings when they learn to relate meaningfully with everything within creation, including the home planet and the vast cosmos. Perhaps our desire to relate is itself one of the deepest explanations of our need for a book like this one, for verbal prayer, using words that express and build these relationships.

Paradox and Pain

In much of the spiritual literature, prayer is described as a struggle—against temptation, distraction, or lack of belief. Trying to get it right with God has been a lifelong endeavor for many contemplative people. Prayer is also linked to suffering and to our attempts to find meaning in suffering, or in spite of it. The role of suffering in our human story and our religious attempts to resolve the dilemma through "redemptive" pain raise awkward questions for modern theology and even more formidable ones for modern spirituality.

Chapter 6 of *Evolutionary Faith* seeks to unravel the quandaries of this complex subject. It highlights one of the major tenets of the new cosmology, and possibly the least understood; namely, that creation evolves according to the twofold paradoxical pattern of Creation and Destruction. Destruction is thus neither an aberration nor an evil; it is an inherent dimension of the cosmic evolutionary process. Pain and destruction are not about creation existing "at a price," nor can they be adequately explained by invoking a central tenet of Darwinian evolution like the survival of the fittest. This is a paradox that defies a one-dimensional rational explanation. Truthfully, it makes sense only in a theological and spiritual context.

A religion like Christianity, centered on the salvific death of the Christ as the ultimate solution to the predicament of suffering, misses the deeper meaning of this paradox. So does the Hindu and Buddhist aspiration to eventual enlightenment, facilitating the escape into Nirvana. There is a quality of suffering, pain, and destruction that is innate and essential to the divine unfolding of creation. What can make the suffering meaningless and unbearable is our human inability—more accurately, our unwillingness—to work creatively with this central paradox. We are forever trying to conquer and control it—and that, more than anything else, is what fuels so much meaningless suffering in our world today.

Meaningless suffering in our world is largely a human problem, requiring a human solution. The supposed fundamental flaw of creation, what the Christian religions call Original Sin, is not a divine problem but a human one. In God's eyes creation is not perfect, but neither is it sinful or evil. It is incomplete and paradoxical.

The Way Out

How do we prayerfully come to terms with this paradox? Currently, we seem to be trapped in a great deal of ignorance and spiritual naiveté. We misunderstand what creation is about, and tragically the formal religions have reinforced that ignorance. Most of our efforts to explain human suffering have actually exacerbated its meaninglessness. The more we try to get rid of it, the more it haunts us. Most of our efforts here seem misguided. The basic problem relates to our inability to see and understand our world in cosmic and planetary terms.

At the root of this problem, it seems to me, is our patriarchal need to dominate and control—one that often reaches epidemic proportions. As a species we need to let go—at several levels. This is not just about acknowledging a divine being as the source of all that exists; it is much more about acknowledging creation's own potential to self-organize, what is called autopoiesis. Only a profound spiritual revolution can bring us to the place of accepting that we humans are not meant to be a dominant but a subservient species, at the service of an organic creative universe.

The prayerfulness required for this shift of heart—and shift of perspective—is essentially that of reclaiming the contemplative, that centered, receptive vulnerability from within which we become porous and transparent to the deep mystery of which we are an integral part. A regular meditation practice will certainly move us in this direction. But it also requires an attitudinal and behavioral change of heart that calls for conversion in several other realms of our daily lives.

Consciousness

Anybody fluent in modern cosmology can scarcely escape an awareness of the bold claim (which I report in Chapter 5 of *Evolutionary Faith*) that consciousness is not merely a feature of the human brain (nor even of the human mind) but primordially belongs to the whole of creation. This is a logical corollary to Fred Hoyle's daring insight of many years ago: that ours is an intelligent universe. This is now a well-established theory, thanks to notions like autopoiesis—the capacity to self-organize—and the Gaia hypothesis (that planet earth should be regarded and treated as an alive organism). Quantum theory also postulates that the universe operates on highly sophisticated laws that often defy the rational analysis of human intelligence.

We are also gathering evidence that suggests that human consciousness is derived from a kind of planetary and cosmic consciousness. Within human awareness, consciousness belongs more to mind than to brain (a distinction first highlighted by anthropologist Gregory Bateson). Mind is thought of as spread throughout the entire body, and not located merely in the brain. Moreover, mind is thought to follow a developmental pattern very different from that of the brain. Mind is imagined as the connective tissue with what psychoanalyst Carl G. Jung called the *collective unconscious,* that creative energy that characterizes the whole of creation. We humans don't evolve the capacity to think; it is probably much more accurate to suggest that we are "thought" into being, that we are the products of thought.

For Jung, the collective unconscious is endowed with light and shadow. Despite its shadow elements, Jung believed that the cosmic energy was divine in its essential nature. In other words, it was not some weird random phenomenon but one endowed with the supreme wisdom that characterizes the ultimate source of meaning itself.

From Here On

For the narrowly rational minds of this age, these may seem pre-posterous claims. They tend to be ridiculed and dismissed as non-sense, even though growing bodies of research in several different disciplines invite us to be favorably disposed to these novel ideas. What seems to be happening is a growing recognition of what the Jesuit paleontologist Teilhard de Chardin predicted many years ago, namely, that our evolution as a human species is virtually complete at a biological level, projecting us on to a new evolu-tionary stage where psychic rather than biological growth will dominate our collective future. In other words, it is the develop-ment of mind and spirit that will come to the fore in our evolu-tion as a species from here on.

Not surprisingly, therefore, we evidenced throughout the latter half of the twentieth century a growing interest in meditation and in ways of praying that were more inner- than outer-focused. Indeed, the rise of the Falun Gong movement in China, posing such a prophetic threat that the Chinese government banned it, torturing and even killing some of its key adherents, is evidence of the power of prophetic silence in the contemporary world. Just as many totalitarian regimes dread the power of the poet, so it seems that several institutions of our time, religious and political, dread the potential of the meditator.

A New Challenge

If these observations are even minimally helpful, then humanity today is faced with an unprecedented spiritual challenge: How do we evaluate and discern the significance of consciousness in our time? The information explosion has increased the desire for knowledge and wisdom, but the subtle evolutionary shift toward mind and spirit may have an even more powerful impact. As a species, we are not ready for this revolution, nor are our religious institutions in any way ready to help us understand what is really going on. Spiritual and cultural enlightenment is probably the most urgent need of our time, with books like this one to help us on our way.

The Australian spiritual writer Michael Morwood, in *Praying a New Story,* offers a useful naming for the spiritual journey confronting humans today. For centuries we were schooled in praying to a God purported to be "elsewhere," in some distant heavenly realm. Now, the Universe Story invites us to pray to a God who is "everywhere." This is the God we encounter in the new cosmology and in many of the explorations of modern science, but it is also the God known to mystics. Our sense of the divine is thus stretched toward enormously expanded horizons.

In several religious contexts, this thought evokes fear of a distant cold, judgmental God, devoid of any real human connection. This fear, I suggest, arises more from anthropocentric perceptions that reduce God to our image and likeness and therefore create barriers to understanding the true God of time and eternity. People who explore God through nature and creation tend not to experience God as cold or distant; indeed, the opposite is often the case. They detect in the wonders and marvels of the natural world an unmistakable closeness of the divine.

Creation Praying in Us

However, here a bigger issue comes to the fore, one that underlies several prayers in the present volume. In the last analysis it is not so much a case of our praying—to or with creation—rather it is a case of creation praying in and through us. Creation, then, becomes the experiential vehicle through which we encounter the divine in a range of different guises. This evokes a new sense of trust and faith because all around us is an awesomely elegant world. The unconditional love of God, which is at the basis of all prayer, comes alive in a new way. From there on, prayer is not so much a skill to be learned, still less a penance to be endured. It becomes one of the most exciting challenges that life calls forth for us.

My trust is that the prayers in this volume will awaken hearts to the contemplative call that God wishes us all to hear. In our knowing of it, and its appropriation in our daily lives, we learn to live differently. We walk gently upon the earth and take time to savor the beauty of creation. Then, perhaps, we will learn to appreciate anew the wonderful creation with which our God has blessed us.

—DIARMUID O'MURCHU

Select Bibliography

Berry, Thomas. *The Dream of the Earth*. San Francisco: Sierra Club Books, 1988.

Berry, Thomas, with Brian Swimme. *The Universe Story: From the Primordial Flaring Forth to the Ecozoic Era—A Celebration of the Unfolding of the Cosmos*. San Fransico: HarperSanFrancisco, 1992.

Haught, John F. *Responses to 101 Questions on God and Evolution*. New York: Paulist, 2001.

———. *Deeper Than Darwin*. Boulder, Colo.: Westview, 2003.

O'Murchu, Diarmuid. *Evolutionary Faith*. Maryknoll, N.Y.: Orbis, 2002. (Principal source and reference.)

———. *Quantum Theology*. Maryknoll, N.Y.: Orbis, 2000.

———. *Religion in Exile*. Maryknoll, N.Y.: Orbis, 2001.

Teilhard de Chardin, Pierre. *The Activation of Energy*. Orlando: Harvest, 2002.

———. *The Divine Milieu*. New York: Harper, 1960.

———. *The Hymn of the Universe*. New York: Harper & Row, 1965.

———. *The Phenomenon of Man*. New York: Harper & Row, 1959.

Index of Prayer Titles

Printed in the USA
CPSIA information can be obtained
at www.ICGtesting.com
JSHW082206140824
68134JS00014B/456